Befriending Our Desires

For Susie

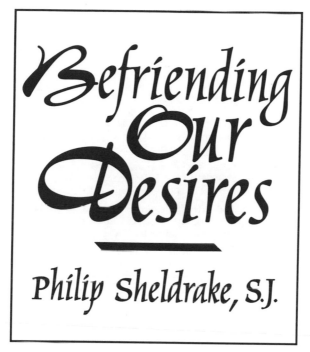

Befriending Our Desires

Philip Sheldrake, S.J.

AVE MARIA PRESS
NOTRE DAME, INDIANA 46556

Philip Sheldrake, S.J., is a Tutor at Westcott House, the Anglican seminary in Cambridge, England, and lecturer in church history and spirituality within the ecumenical Cambridge Theological Federation. He is also part-time general editor of *The Way* journal, which is based at Heythrop College, London.

Excerpt from"Burnt Norton" in *Collected Poems 1909-1962* by T.S. Eliot. Copyright © 1936 by Harcourt Brace & Company, copyright © 1964, 1963 by T.S. Eliot, reprinted by permission of the publisher.

Excerpts reprinted from *The Complete Works*, Hadewijch, translated by Mother Columba Hart. Copyright © 1981 by the Missionary Society of St. Paul the Apostle in the State of New York. Used by permission of Paulist Press.

Excerpts from *An Interrupted Life*, Etty Hillesum, translated by Arno Pomerans. English translation copyright © 1983 by Jonathan Cape Ltd., copyright © 1981 by De Hann/Uniboek b.v. Bussum. Reprinted by permission of Pantheon Books, a division of Random House.

Excerpts reprinted from *Julian of Norwich: Showings*, translated by Edmun Colledge, O.S.A., and James Walsh, S.J. Copyright © 1978 by the Missionary Society of St. Paul the Apostle in the State of New York. Used by permission of Paulist Press.

Excerpts from *The New Jerusalem Bible*, copyright © 1985 by Darton, Longman & Todd, Ltd. and Doubleday & Company, Inc. Reprinted by permission of the publisher.

© 1994 by Ave Maria Press, Inc., Notre Dame, IN 46556

International Standard Book Number: 0-87793-537-8

0-87793-536-X (pbk.)

Library of Congress Catalog Card Number: 94-71729

Cover and text design by Katherine Robinson Coleman

Cover photograph by Jean-Claude LeJeune

Printed and bound in the United States of America.

Contents

Through desires of unquiet love
The soul can win no repose,
And through desires of strong love
It loses repose and inner quiet.
So it drowns in sublime Love,
And so it finds its unattainable desire nearby;
For anyone in misery cannot find contentment
Unless desire can be fulfilled;
For desire comes from such a lofty nature,
It cannot be at rest in any small thing.
Love flees, and desire follows hard after,
And never finds a resting place.

—*Hadewijch, "Poems in Couplets," 10.*

Preface

Many of the great Christian spiritual teachers have used "desire," "yearning," "longing" or equivalents, as central metaphors for our search for God and, indeed, for God's reaching out toward humanity. And yet I and, without doubt, many other people were not brought up to think of desire as a possible key to the spiritual journey. It was more natural to view our desires in purely bodily terms or as indicators of personal willfulness. These were problems not easy to integrate into our understanding of Christian faith.

This book has grown out of a growing conviction that it is vitally important to recover a spirituality of desire. Only by attending to our desires are we able to encounter our deepest self—the image of God within us. I want to illustrate in an accessible rather than scholarly way how the Christian spiritual tradition has a great deal to say about desire—in relation to prayer, God, choice and discernment. Finally, it is obviously true that desire is also associated with our sexuality. The Christian community is only slowly recovering a sense that sexuality and spirituality are inextricably linked.

In terms of the whole project, I owe particular thanks to my classes at the Retreats International Summer Institute at the University of Notre Dame, which have helped me to formulate many of the ideas in this book. The ordinands at Westcott House, Cambridge, have also had to listen to me in class and in chapel addresses as I struggled to develop my ideas on desire further! Finally, the chapter on sexuality could not have been written without the regular help of several close friends, married, single and celibate. However, I take responsibility for the final wording!

Both Frank Cunningham of Ave Maria Press and Morag Reeve at Darton, Longman and Todd have been encouraging and supportive throughout.

The scripture quotations cited are taken from the New Jerusalem Bible. A list of other works that are quoted in the book, mainly primary sources in English translation, appears at the end. The modern English editions of major spiritual texts in *The Classics of Western Spirituality* series, published by Paulist Press, are a wonderful resource for all of us who teach and study spirituality.

> Philip Sheldrake
> Cambridge 1994

ONE

A Spirituality of Desire?

"Our desire must be like a slow and stately ship, sailing across endless oceans, never in search of safe anchorage" (Hillesum 1985, 92).

> Abruptly, Florence asked, "Is there nothing that you long for quite passionately? *Want?*"
>
> "Oh, all human beings have aspirations!"
>
> "Aspirations! I was not talking of anything so elevated. *Wants....* Desires."
>
> Florence looked round the garden wildly. It was cold and almost dark and the rain had begun again. In the buildings behind them, she felt the presence of studious, purposeful, dedicated young women.
>
> "This ..." she gestured. "I could never aspire to this."
>
> Nor ever want it, she realized. For the air would surely suffocate her (Hill 1992, 60).

Although those of us who live there may know otherwise, the rarefied atmosphere of Cambridge University colleges and their aspirations, so deftly captured in Susan Hill's novel *Air and Angels*, appears to be the complete opposite of the perpetual movement of Etty Hillesum's desires. Ancient universities seem more at home with ideals and elevated emotions than with mere human needs or the uncertainty of

desire! But one of the novel's characters, Florence, has more
down to earth feelings that appear to be beyond the grasp of
her friend Thea, a university teacher, as they share afternoon
tea. For, although she cannot afford to admit it too explicitly,
Florence desires Thomas Cavendish, the irreproachable cler-
gyman, and is seeking some way, from whatever source, to
achieve her end.

A similar contrast between, on the one hand, the earthi-
ness and concrete quality of desires, wants, longings or passions and, on the other, more elevated ideals and emotions
has also been common in Christian thinking. In popular
presentations of Christian history, it is the elevated, apparently more "spiritual" values, rather than the earthy, that have
come to be associated with the dedication, purpose and
virtue of serious believers or aspiring saints.

Conventional images of holiness do not encourage us to
befriend our desires. Indeed, they usually suggest that saints,
if they ever showed signs of having personal desires at all,
soon lose them in some overwhelming conversion experience. In Hill's novel it is true that Florence's desire is not
a very healthy one but has the quality of obsession and
possessiveness. Not all desire is, however, of this sort. The
problem is that unless we feel free to own our desires in the
first place, we will never learn how to recognize those that
are more fruitful and healthy, let alone how to live out of the
deepest desires of all.

To my mind, desire is intimately associated with our
capacity to love truly—ourselves, other people, God and
even more abstract things such as ideals or causes. Love, we
need to remember, is not simply a matter of immediate
feelings. There may be times, even in the most intense love
commitments, when tangible feelings are absent. But love
ultimately proves itself in its focused attention and its quality
of dedication, which is richer and deeper than mere duty or
will power. It is perhaps what St. Augustine means by "in-
tention" and the author of the English medieval text *The
Cloud of Unknowing*, by "naked intent."

Desires or Ideals?

Unfortunately, where human love has been allowed any role in traditional Christian spirituality, it had to be the spiritual, disinterested, universal love of agape rather than the engaged, passionate, particular love of eros. These have been treated as two distinct kinds of love. Indeed, they have been viewed in hierarchical terms as a higher love and a lower love. Only agape was commonly associated with God and therefore godliness, even though, as we shall see, eros played an important role in the thinking of some significant figures such as Meister Eckhart.

I well recall a letter to a church newspaper some years ago concerning the writer's difficulties with the more homely and personal style of worship that had been introduced into his local parish. "After all, Jesus asked us to *love* our neighbors not to *like* them!" We will probably also recall the old adage, "as cold as charity." A more contemporary update I heard recently from an American friend described a superficial type of generosity in graphic terms—"As wide as the Rio Grande and just as shallow." It is all too easy for a so-called universal, disinterested agape love to be simply *un*interested and well protected. A gift of everything but myself. Donation without commitment. A recent article in a well-respected British religious weekly noted that too many clergy appear able to relate to their parishioners only in this disengaged way. The writer rather sharply affirmed that she had no wish to be the object of someone's universal love! As I hope will become clear throughout this book, I believe that the radical separation of agape love from eros love is a very unhelpful way of seeing things.

For present purposes, however, it is fair to say that human desires have a particular association with eros love, or "erotic power," and are feelings of attraction toward or aversion from objects, people and ideas. Any desire is essentially personal, that is to say, associated with the kind of person we are. However, it can be directed toward nonpersonal things such as material possessions or abstract qualities such as success, justice and perfection. The point is that desire is not some kind of impersonal power "out there" that controls us whether we like it or not. Desires are best understood as our most honest experiences of ourselves, in all our complexity and depth, as we relate to people and things around us. Desires are not the same as instincts— either human ones or those of other animals. Although desires have sometimes had a bad press, being more or less reduced to the instinctual, they in fact involve a reflective element. They are therefore, as far as we know, uniquely human qualities. In particular, we need to rescue *desire* from attempts to reduce its meaning to sexual libido and its increasingly murky associations with abuse or sexual power games.

On the other hand, desires undoubtedly overlap with our needs and neediness, although it is still possible to distinguish between them. Both may be conscious or unconscious. In fact, it is not unusual to experience a conflict between our conscious and unconscious levels. As we reflect on our lives we can come to understand more clearly how unconscious needs have the capacity to drive us to behave in ways that we actually dislike or which fail to express our truest self. For example, we may be driven by a deeply buried need to succeed, and to be seen to succeed, while on a conscious level we say to ourselves and to others how much we *desire* to operate differently! When we choose to talk of befriending desires rather than simply responding to needs, we are implying that desires involve a positive and active reaching out to something or someone. Such a movement goes beyond our temporary reactions to immediate circumstances and actually touches upon deeper questions of our identity and our ideals.

Thus, to return to my comments on Susan Hill's novel, if we distinguish desires from aspirations it is not because desires have nothing to do with *ideals*, for they frequently do. It is simply that desires have a more grounded quality than what we generally understand by aspirations. Desires are more intrinsic to the reality of each person. True and realistic ideals have this same intrinsic quality. Aspirations, on the other hand, often speak rather more of *idealization*, of something outside ourselves, indeed detached from our own experience and capacities, but against which we feel we should measure our life. If this is the case, we can think of desire as an openness to the fullness of *what is* rather than to *what ought to be*. Desires, then, contrast with a world of duties or of unrealistic dreams. Any ideal that attempts to overcome desire and replace it with cool reason is both inhuman and unattainable.

Whether most of us are aware of it or not, the early centuries of the Christian community set the tone for much that came afterward and which still influences us. Not least has been the powerful effect of various ascetical trends inherited from the pre-Christian classical era. These presented the ideal human being as free from need and desire—especially our apparently inescapable dependencies on food and sex. Because desire has a grounded quality it is inevitably linked to our physical senses, which in turn connect us to the world of time and space. In a way, all desire is *sensual*, that is, associated with our senses. It is interesting that we instinctively make this connection when we talk of "being sensible" about taking wise actions or making wise choices. We also speak of arriving at a more healthy way of seeing and doing as "coming to our senses."

The Power of Desire

In general, our desire is a powerful matter. Individual desires, like all feelings, vary in intensity. They can range from faint wishes to powerful passions that drive us in particular directions and govern our thoughts and actions. Some are fleeting while others last longer and reappear repeatedly. But the main point is that there is nothing passive or limp about desire, for it gives energy and direction to our psyche.

I discovered this for myself in a fairly straightforward way when I was finally able to give up smoking after some twenty-five years. I had known for a long time that it would be a sensible thing to do and, in that sense, I hoped for it. The problem was that on another level I still found that the enjoyment of smoking outweighed my sense of abusing my body and therefore myself. And so every effort to give up broke down after days or weeks. This went on for several years until finally, during a period of sabbatical leave, I said, "I do not *want* to smoke. I positively *desire* to stop. I am going to stop." And somewhat to my amazement, I did stop. This was not a question of sheer will power, let alone great virtue! Even more surprising, the experience was relatively painless. There were only a few days of mild withdrawal and very little gritting of my teeth. I do not mean to cheapen the much tougher struggle with such addictions that others have had to go through. My point is simply that until giving up smoking moved from being a vague aspiration to touching the deeper level of myself where the power of desire could be unleashed nothing much happened. When it did touch that level, the focused strength of desire had the capacity to enable me to change behavior.

The fourteenth-century Italian mystic Catherine of Siena recognized this positive and extraordinary power of our desires when she wrote that it makes them one of the few ways of touching God: "You have nothing infinite except your soul's love and desire" (*Dialogue*, 270). The German Dominican mystic of the same period, Meister Eckhart, suggested that the reason we are not able to see God is the faintness of our desire. In the graceful language of desire that permeates Archbishop Thomas Cranmer's *Book of Common Prayer*, one of the foundation documents of the English Reformation, there is a difference between following "too much the devices and desires of our own hearts" and the "holy desires," "good counsels" and "just works" that proceed only from God's inspiration. Yet, even holy desires—the desires that ultimately find their rest and quietness only in God—tap into energies that are partially physical.

The sensual, indeed sexual quality (understood properly) of even holy desires is witnessed to by the language of many of the great Christian mystics. This is something to which I shall return later. The problem is that if we have frequently been taught to understand the spiritual life as mainly, if not exclusively, about *giving up* things, we may never hear the call to engage with life or particular issues in a passionate way. Attention to desire, on the other hand, is about cultivating in ourselves that capacity for passionate concern. Because desire is such a strong thing there is always a hint of risk. We are probably aware that some desires may enslave us, others dissipate our energies. But desire can generate power and physical energy and may also galvanize our spirituality. The fact that we frequently do not allow ourselves such risks and so often lack a lively spirituality has close connections with the frequent absence of a serious and healthy theology of the Holy Spirit in Western Christianity.

This problem goes far beyond the presence or absence of a few dramatic manifestations of "charismatic" gifts. The Spirit blowing where it wills is the risky, wild and profligate side of God inviting us to seek a similar risky freedom and to pour ourselves out into situations, commitments and relationships. The Spirit is vulnerable as well as powerful. To allow ourselves actively to desire is also to be vulnerable. The Spirit of God given to us does not simply lead us into all truth but also into the vulnerability of Jesus' way. But to take such risks is at the same time to know ourselves to be held securely and to be safe at some deep and essential level beyond our own powers to control. The Spirit is also the indwelling power of God in the heart of each of us, sustaining us.

Should I Have Desires?

On several occasions I have been struck by two common reactions from people I have taught in classes on the spirituality of desire. These somehow sum up the human and spiritual dilemma. The first is, "I have so many desires that I don't know what to do with them." Without doubt such a feeling is partly related to our fears and sense that we lack control over our inner life. But the variety of desires is also confusing. This makes our experience of desire appear ambiguous with no reliable means of distinguishing between the superficial and the deep, the healthy and the unhealthy. There are certainly many conflicts that we shall have to face if we decide to take our desires seriously. Perhaps we are tempted to feel that it would be safer to treat them all with equal suspicion and to try to live (at least in our better moments) in reference to more objective values.

The second reaction goes something along these lines. "I was taught not to have desires ... or, rather, I was given the message from childhood onward that it was important to fulfill the desires of certain other important people in my life." So, even more powerful than the *oughts* and *shoulds* of objective values were the people in reference to whose desire or will we were taught to live. These might be parents, teachers, our spouse, the church and, most powerfully of all, God. The teaching of the Christian church has tended to place a very strong emphasis on external sources of authority in contrast to our personal desires. Desire was felt to suggest private judgement and the uncontrollable. To follow our desires seemed like a failure in obedience to church norms in favor of self-will. Duty, faithfulness to the expectations of others, or self-denial in an almost literal sense of denying individual personality and tastes all too easily became the criteria for spiritual progress—often to the detriment of physical and psychological health in the long term. Because desire suggests passion, a person of "good judgment" was often thought to be cool and objective. It seemed, therefore, that desire should not guide our choices so much as a cultivated detachment from any strong (and implicitly, unreliable) feelings.

In his *Spiritual Exercises* the sixteenth-century founder of the Society of Jesus, Ignatius Loyola, invites any person who makes a retreat to "ask God our Lord for what I want and desire" at the beginning of every period of prayer. Many people find that their unconscious response is to exclaim, "What *I* desire? I have no desires!" Or, we say to God, rather prematurely, "I want what *you* want!" We find ourselves stuck—instinctively mouthing the "appropriate" feeling or the truly spiritual aspiration! While it is true that today the language of co-dependency and addiction is sometimes used too glibly in spirituality circles, there is some truth in admitting a condition of spiritual addiction that leads us to fulfil the desires of others (even a God created in the image of human authority figures) in a compulsive way with a consequent erosion of our own identity.

Desire and God

As a consequence I, and many other Christians I have met over the years, have found it hard to think of desire as a key to the spiritual journey. On the contrary, desire is experienced as a problem or at least as something difficult to integrate with our understanding and practice of faith. This is partly because we have inherited an image of a very disengaged God. Consequently, we do not instinctively relate to the more biblical notion of a God who is passionately engaged with the whole of creation, whose life is a continuous movement out of self, who is God precisely as the one who out of love sends the Son into our world not to condemn it but to redeem it. As Jon Sobrino and other Latin American liberation theologians have reminded us, the cross of Christ is not just an event or an act but in a radical way points to the nature of God's being.

On the cross of Jesus God himself is crucified. The
Father suffers the death of the Son and takes upon
himself all the pain and suffering of history. In this
ultimate solidarity with humanity he reveals himself
as the God of love, who opens up a hope and a future
through the most negative side of history. Thus,
Christian existence is nothing else but a process of
participating in this same process whereby God loves
the world, and hence in the very life of God (Sobrino
1978, 224).

Unfortunately, a more familiar influence in the consciousness of many Christians is the image of a passionless,
detached God whose perfection (based partly on the view of
the universe of the Greek philosopher Aristotle) is to be
self-contained, still and at rest. According to this image,
God's will is eternal, predetermined and extrinsic to our own
hopes and feelings. If we believe ourselves to be created in
the image of *that* God, we can easily associate desire and
passion with lack of balance, confusion, loss of control and
dangerous subjectivity. Desire is also closely linked to
sexuality, which seems to have little to do with common
(traditional male?) perceptions of the spiritual. Desire, then,
is too often viewed with suspicion as something disturbing
or misleading, even if pleasurable, rather than something to
be embraced as a positive and dynamic force. As a consequence, human love for God has been treated for centuries
as unique, disconnected from all other forms of human
loving.

Despite the power of all this psychological and spiritual
inheritance, I want to suggest that spirituality is in fact intimately associated with desire—our own and God's.
Human longing for fulfillment in God does not need to be
based on our denigration of other forms of love that connect
us with created reality. On the contrary, all of them are
interconnected. For this reason we can validly talk of "erotic"
elements in our love of God. This does not necessarily in-

volve us in using explicitly *sexual* imagery, although the
evidence from many of the classic Christian mystics is that it
may sometimes do so. But we understand the word *erotic*
more broadly as that passionate, specific and partly physical
energy that lies behind other human loves and deep commitments. In that case desire is inevitably bound up with our
relationship with God. The highest form of love, drawing us
into a more perfect relationship with God, includes rather
than excludes the best in all our human experiences of love.

Many of the great spiritual teachers used desire or its
equivalents as the central metaphor for the human search for
God or for God's search for humanity. Other writers speak
of befriending our desires as vital to spiritual growth and
discernment. As we shall observe throughout this book,
people like Augustine, Gregory of Nyssa, the medieval
monks with their liking for the Song of Songs, the Beguine
Hadewijch, Bonaventure, Eckhart, Catherine of Siena, Julian
of Norwich, the author of *The Cloud of Unknowing*, the great
Carmelites Teresa of Avila and John of the Cross, Ignatius
Loyola, George Herbert, Thomas Traherne and the Wes-
leys—to name but a few—in their different ways preached a
religion of desire.

The foundation of Christian tradition is, of course, the
scriptures. Both Hebrew and Christian scriptures are full of
the themes of desire, yearning and longing. The writers of
the psalms were never afraid to express deep and powerful
emotions of this kind in relation to God:

As a deer yearns for running streams,
so I yearn for you, my God.
I thirst for God, the living God;
when shall I go to see the face of God? (Psalm 42:1-2).

God, too, is a God who desires us and yearns for us:

Yahweh is tenderness and pity,
slow to anger and rich in faithful love.
As tenderly as a father treats his children,
so Yahweh treats those who fear him (Psalm 103:8,13).

The consoling prophecy of Second Isaiah to the defeated and exiled people of Israel portrays God's desire as so great that the people's image or name is carved into the palm of God's hand:

Zion was saying,
    "Yahweh has abandoned me,
    the Lord has forgotten me."
Can a woman forget her baby at the breast,
feel no pity for the child she has borne?
Even if these forget, I shall not forget you.
Look, I have engraved you on the palms of my hands
    (Isaiah 49:14-16).

But desire and longing are not only for God. The Gospel of Matthew links desire to the author's great theme of justice in the Beatitudes: "Blessed are those who hunger and thirst for uprightness [or justice]; they shall have their fill" (Matthew 5:6). Chapter 10 of the Gospel of Mark highlights the different qualities and intensities of human desires. The rich man certainly desires to be good and to love God (vv. 17-22), but he also wants material security and familiar surroundings. The scriptures here do not present a crude contrast between love of God and love of other things and people. Rather, the point is that the man's deepest desire for God, and all that this implied, was still not free to find full expression. The sons of Zebedee (vv. 35-40) desire to be with Jesus but also seek the status and power that they believe the Kingdom of God will bring to them. To desire fully to be with Jesus is to allow ourselves to risk sharing in who Jesus really is and thus in a process of stripping away our more superficial desires. The blind beggar, Bartimaeus (vv. 46-52), contrasts strongly with the spiritual blindness of both the rich man and the disciples. His deep, intensely focused and active desire is not merely to be healed but, as with the previous cases, to follow Jesus. In this case, singleness of desire brings both healing and following.

Authentic Desires

I think it is important to realize that while all desires are real experiences, not all are equally authentic in the sense of expressions of our authentic selves. Certain desires spring from a more profound level of ourselves than others. Depth of desire is not necessarily the same as intensity of feeling. For example, violence or abuse of various kinds can result in a strong and immediate desire for revenge. This is natural and understandable. Yet, as Christians, we would want to say that ultimately we need to move beyond that level of desire to a deeper, more authentic level where the power of forgiveness can be found. Authentic desires come from our essential selves rather than from the surface of our personalities or from our immediate reactions to situations and experiences. Such authentic desires tend to reach into the very heart of our identities. At this level the questions "Who am I?" and "What do I want?" touch intimately upon each other. To return to the teaching of Ignatius Loyola, "to ask God our Lord for what I want and desire" as we focus our prayer is an invitation to us to acknowledge our immediate sense of need. But this is only a starting point for the gradual unfolding of that with which we are most passionately and deeply engaged. Our great desire is sometimes well hidden beneath a confusing mass of more insistent wants, needs and longings. To move through the various levels of desire clearly demands discernment. This is such an important subject that I will dedicate a chapter to it later.

So, the more honestly we try to identify our authentic desires, the more we can identify who we truly are. We can think of our authentic desires as vocational in orientation. They can be guides to what we are called to become, to live and to do. If we want to begin to know who others are beyond the externals of their immediate life stories, we need to understand their desires, which find expression in words and actions. Of course, we all display more immediately the desires that express more superficial aspects of ourselves. But ultimately a pattern of what we want in and from life emerges and thus provides one of the best clues to the true self. If our desires reveal who we are, then one value of attending to them is that it helps us gradually to see our true self behind the masks we wear. At the same time it helps us to become what God desires us to be as expressed in the process of our very creation. This was the level of experience probed in the three stories of Mark 10. And that is, it seems to me, one of the points of Jesus' question to the disciples of John the Baptist in the opening chapter of John's Gospel: "What do you want?" (John 1:38). It is a question of "What do you want your life to be? Who do you really think you are?" The disciples' response is to ask Jesus, "Where do you live?" That may seem a rather odd response on the face of it. However, place is not merely geographical but also a question of a person's place in the world, in the scheme of things. The response indicates a desire to come to know their "place" and where and how they should live in relation to Jesus' "place."

The more authentic our desires, the more they touch upon our identities and also upon the reality of God at the heart of our being. Our most authentic desires spring ultimately from the deep inner wells where the longing for God runs freely. This is so even if the desires are not always expressed in explicitly religious terms. Our deepest desires, therefore, to some degree move us beyond self-centeredness to self-giving. To put it another way, these desires are not narrowly concerned with ourselves but with the growth of the Kingdom of God. They reflect God's own desires, God's longing for the world as well as for each of us particularly. In this sense, authentic desires have a social or collective dimension.

There is obviously something of a paradox here. I have said that deep desires reflect what is uniquely personal. Yet, at the same time, the more deeply we go into ourselves, the more surely these desires are seen to transcend individualism. At the level of deep desires, any distinction between what we desire and the desires with which God gifts us actually begins to blur. The more profoundly we reach into ourselves the more we experience desires that are *both* uniquely our own and also uniquely God-given. I think it is important to affirm at this point that these remarks are true of healthy sexual desire as well. The quality of our sexual desire is a sort of paradigm of the kind of people we are and cannot, therefore, be distinguished from other sorts of desire.

Toward a Spirituality of Desire

Given all that I have so far said, my hope in the remainder of this book is to explore in a broad and accessible way a spirituality of desire in order to show that it is only by attending to desires that we may encounter our deepest self, the image of God, within. I believe that the degree to which we value or devalue human desire as the key to our inner growth, as well as growth in relation to other people or the world around us, depends very much on our images of God. It is to this issue that I propose to turn my attention first. There are two key questions. Is God a God of desire? The seventeenth-century Anglican priest and mystic Thomas Traherne had no doubts that God is. Traherne is one of the most striking and beautiful spiritual writers on the subject of desire—ours and God's. "His wants put a lustre upon his enjoyments and make them infinite" (*Centuries*, 1.44). Second, if we say that the goal of all human desire is God, does this mean that all other desires are a distraction or that God is to be found at the heart of all desire? I suggest that a thoroughly Christian, incarnational answer is the second.

Following closely on the heels of a consideration of healthy or distorted images of God comes the question of our explicit relationship with God, or what we call prayer. In the Christian tradition, it is not only Ignatius Loyola who considered that our desire should become focused in prayer and indeed become an important aspect of growth in prayer. Desire, or its equivalents, plays a major role in the approach to prayer taught by many spiritually enlightened people from the desert fathers and mothers to a number of the great Western mystics. People often think of desert monasticism in terms of unattractive asceticism. However, while it is clearly true that there were dubious exaggerations, a healthy asceticism was actually an effective discipline to focus desire more sharply. As Abba Joseph said to Abba Lot, "You cannot be a monk unless you become like a consuming fire." On another occasion he said to Lot, with his fingers "like ten lamps of fire...If you will, you can become all flame" (Ward 1975, 103).

Some spiritual writers mention a deepening of desire in association with the gradual loss of images of God. The inability to pin God down, as it were, to this or that image drives us ultimately into a certain darkness or unknowing in which desire alone becomes the force that drives us onward. It is sometimes important to remind ourselves that dryness in prayer is not the same as absence of desire—in fact the contrary is true. For Julian of Norwich, "longing" or "yearning" are key experiences not only in our forgiveness by God and conversion from sin but also in our developing relationship to God. And for the anonymous author of *The Cloud of Unknowing*, "Now you have to stand in desire all your life long" (Chapter 2). In other words, we need to stand open-handed and openhearted, not assuming that we know best or, indeed, that we know anything. We need also to learn how to wait and, like Mary in the Lucan story of the annunciation, ask continually, "How can this be?" Waiting is one of the hardest lessons for the serious seeker after God. By standing in desire we need to be ready to struggle and to allow our perspectives to change so that we are ever more open to God's action in us.

Delight, play and pleasure are not concepts that many of us instinctively associate with holiness, the search for God or spirituality. We may admit that the word *desire* has some kind of spiritual dimension but its passionate sexual connotations seem to lack the sober quality needed among sound and serious seekers. Is it not the case that from Buddhist ascetics to Christian contemplatives a culture of celibacy has predominated? This culture affects the self-understanding of even those Christians who have not opted for celibate lifestyles. So, the question of the relationship among desire, intimacy and sexuality needs to be addressed. It is not merely a question of asking how we can be spiritual with all the distractions of family and wage-earning. An even sharper question is: How can sexuality *be* spiritual experience as opposed to something that, at the very least, is spiritually confusing or, at worst, some kind of loss of innocence and of our essential energies?

Our desires imply a condition of incompleteness because they speak to us of what we are not or what we do not have. Desire is also, therefore, a condition of openness to possibility and to the future. Desires may ground us in the present moment, but at the same time they point to the fact that this moment does not contain all the answers. Clearly, such ideas have a great deal to do with our experience of choice and change. Being people of desire implies a process of continually choosing. Here, once again, desire comes into its own as the condition for discerning what our choices are and then choosing from within the self rather than according to extrinsic demands. Discernment may be thought of as a journey through desires—a process whereby we move from a multitude of desires, or from surface desires, to our deepest desire which, as it were, *contains* all that is true and vital about ourselves.

This is a process of inclusion rather than exclusion. The movement inward is where the essential self, or image of God within, may be encountered. Yet this journey also involves engaging with the ambiguities of desire. Initially we are aware of many, sometimes contradictory desires. How are we to recognize the level of deepest desire that truly includes all that we *are*? For the mystics Meister Eckhart and Julian of Norwich that which is evil or destructive or sinful, and which is excluded, is in the end nothing, "no-thing." All that is good and has meaning is part of what we mean by deepest desire because it is part of ourselves and part of God. At the heart of all of us is a center that is a point of intersection where our deepest desire and God's desiring in us meet and are found to coincide.

Being people of desire also means that we live within a condition of constant change rather than experience occasional changes from one static situation to another. Our spiritual journeys are essentially stories of continual transition. In this way, desire may become a metaphor for transformation.

If desire is our openness to possibility and a metaphor for change, and if we say that to be human is to desire, how do we relate these things to traditional Christian images of perfection, the vision of God and eternal life? Surely these have a very static quality, because they imply completion and our final possession of all that matters. The afterlife as a condition of "eternal rest" has been assumed to involve freedom from desire first because there is no need for "more" and second because the sexual connotations of desire are assumed to be overtaken by union with God. In this regard, Jesus' comment to the Sadducees that "at the resurrection men and women do not marry; no, they are like the angels in heaven" (Matthew 22:30) has been asked to carry more meaning than it can validly bear. Of course, none of us can possibly know what eternal life will ultimately mean. But against the traditional static view I suggest that it may, like the God we encounter, have an eternally dynamic quality in which we shall remain beings of desire.

> For giving me desire,
> An eager thirst, a burning ardent fire,
> A virgin infant flame,
> A love with which into the world I came,
> An inward hidden heavenly love,
> Which in my soul did work and move,
> And ever ever me inflame,
> With restless longing heavenly avarice,

That never could be satisfied,
That did incessantly a Paradise
Unknown suggest, and something undescried
Discern, and bear me to it; be
Thy name for ever prais'd by me (Traherne 1991,
     "Desire").

TWO

Desire and God

> You must want like a God that you may be satisfied
> like God. Were you not made in his image...? His
> wants are as lively as his enjoyments: always present
> with him. For his life is perfect and he feels them both.
> His wants put a lustre upon his enjoyments and make
> them infinite (Thomas Traherne, *Centuries*, 1.44).

I was certainly not brought up to think of God in terms of
wants, needs or desires. In one sense the strongly sacramental Catholicism of my youth did suggest an intimate God—
particularly one who fed us in the regular reception of holy
communion. If I leave aside the sterner admonitions of the
visiting preachers during the annual parish mission, God
was usually spoken of as loving. And yet this love was
mainly to be seen in God's mercy for us repentant sinners.
This mercy cast a veil over God's otherwise strong natural
inclination to impart justice! At the very best there was an
ambiguity about God's closeness to us. At worst, the ritual,
the hierarchy around the altar, the screens that separated us
as laity, suggested a fundamental divide between our world
and God's home, our experience and God's way of being.

29

God's Wants

"You must want like a God." The seventeenth-century Anglican mystic Thomas Traherne offers quite a contrast. For him, our human desire *is* the image of God within us. It is God operating in us and gifting us with a holy dissatisfaction with anything transitory or less than all. Traherne seems to use "desire" and "wants" interchangeably and to understand both as our openness to infinity. "Wants are the bands and cement between God and us. Had we not wanted we could never have been obliged. Whereas now we are infinitely obliged because we want infinitely" (*Centuries*, 1.51). God is very much a God of desire. Indeed, for Traherne, God could not be God without desire because "want is the fountain of all His fullness." For, "had there been no need He would not have created the world, nor made us, nor manifested His wisdom nor exercised His power, nor beautified eternity, nor prepared the Joys of Heaven" (*Centuries*, 1.42).

Unfamiliar as it may seem, Thomas Traherne is not alone in the Christian spiritual tradition in linking desire and God. The fourteenth-century Rhineland mystic Meister Eckhart is full of references to the connection between God's outpouring of love in creation and incarnation and God's eternal reality. In one of his Latin sermons, designated for the first Sunday after Trinity, Meister Eckhart speaks of God giving "himself without thinking about his loving, but as the sun shines forth." It is of God's nature to love. Therefore, we should "not thank God because he loves us—he must do so! But I thank God because he is so good that he must love" (*Latin Sermon*, VI). In another sermon Eckhart suggests "that the soul is touched immediately by the Holy Spirit because in the love in which God loves himself he also loves me.... And if this love did not exist in which God loves the soul, the Holy Spirit would not exist" (*German Sermons*, 10). For Meister Eckhart, this implies that God's act of creating in love is a permanent state. In other words, God is so filled with love that God is, as it were, continually being born in the soul, the welcoming space at the heart of every person. All that is needed on our part is "humility," that is, openness to receiving the mystery:

> If a man humbles himself, God cannot withhold his own goodness but must come down and flow into the humble man. What God gives is his being, and his being is his goodness, and his goodness is his love (*German Sermon,* 22).

For Meister Eckhart (see his *Latin Sermon,* VI) the love with which God loves humanity *is* the same mutual love that unites the Trinity. God's love for us is itself a sharing in the divine life. God's love is also identified in human experience with the Spirit. "He loves us in such a way that it is as if his blessedness depended on it." And, finally, "he gives himself and everything he has."

The fourteenth-century English mystic Julian of Norwich's favorite word for our desires and God's is "longing."

> For as truly as there is in God a quality of pity and compassion, so truly is there in God a quality of thirst and longing: and the power of this longing in Christ enables us to respond to his longing, and without this no soul comes to heaven. And this quality of longing and thirst comes from God's everlasting goodness (*Showings*, chapter 31).

She goes on to describe the focus of God's love: "God's thirst is to have man, generally, drawn into him" (chapter 75). In other words, God's fundamental desire is that we are to become united with God and to share in God's own "bliss." As with Eckhart, the quality of God's longing is not something accidental but is part of God's very nature from all eternity. One might say that as God's being is eternal, and as longing is natural to God, so God's creativity and God's outpouring in love also exists from all eternity and for all eternity. Perhaps, incidentally, there may be a bridge here from the Christian mystical tradition to one of the postulates of the new cosmology, which suggests that while the universe is finite it has no beginning in time.

Incarnation and Cross

The understanding that desire in God is an eternal quality is implicitly reinforced in rather less poetic terms than in Eckhart or Julian by the sixteenth-century founder of the Jesuits, Ignatius Loyola, in his "Contemplation on the Incarnation" from the *Spiritual Exercises*. The three divine persons gaze,

> on the whole surface or circuit of the world, full of people; and ... seeing that they were all going down into hell they decide in their eternity that the Second Person should become a human being, in order to save the human race (no. 102).

This image of course links God's eternal love not only with the incarnation but also with the cross of Jesus. The passion of Jesus is not simply God's reaction to the fallen condition of humanity. Neither incarnation nor redemption is, strictly speaking, forced upon God. Our own experience is that to long for something *is* to anguish and at times to suffer spiritual pain. Equally, there is an inherent connection between God's eternal longing and the agony of suffering for the one loved, which is expressed in the cross of Jesus. At the end of the *Spiritual Exercises* Ignatius Loyola invites us to reflect further on the eternal quality of God's desire for us in relation to divine self-giving and indwelling in all things and people:

> I will ponder with deep affection how much God our Lord has done for me, and how much he has given me of what he possesses, and consequently how he, the same Lord, desires to give me his very self, in accordance with his divine design (no. 234).

For another sixteenth-century Spanish mystic, Teresa of Avila, the fact of Christ sharing our human experience is an incarnation of the desire of God to be with us in our weakness and vulnerability. God, in Christ, knows our neediness and that we could not begin to move toward God without the faithful presence of Christ. The eucharist, for Teresa, is where we continue to encounter the divine desire to be unconditionally available to us:

> Seeing our need, therefore, the good Jesus has sought the admirable means whereby He has shown us the extreme love which He has for us, and in His own name and in that of His brethren He has made this petition. "Give us Lord, this day our daily bread."

> What a great love is that of the Son and what a great love is that of the Father! Yes, for He is not like us; knowing that He was carrying out His words by loving us as He loves Himself, He went about seeking how He could carry out this commandment more perfectly, even at His own cost (*The Way of Perfection,* chapter 33).

The notion that God desires us implies that, in some sense, God *needs* us, and this is a much more difficult notion for us to grasp and accept. In one of his most direct and radical statements about the love of God, Meister Eckhart preached,

> Know that God loves the soul so powerfully that it staggers the mind. If one were to deprive God of this so that he did not love the soul, one would deprive him of his life and being, or one would kill God if we may say such a thing. For that same love by which God loves the soul is his life, and in this same love the Holy Spirit blossoms forth; and this same love *is* the Holy Spirit (*German Sermons,* 69).

Gospel of Luke

The parable of the so-called prodigal son in the Gospel of Luke hints at something of the same idea of God. Although the three stories in chapter 15 of the gospel are usually referred to as parables of God's mercy, they might equally be understood as parables of the desire that is part of God's nature. It is the power of this desire that breaks through human barriers such as those proposed by the Pharisees and scribes (v. 2). In the story of the efforts of the shepherd to retrieve one lost sheep, God rejoices in the "wastefulness" of love. God's desire is shown to be focused on each person particularly and equally, however illogical that may seem. Then God is compared to a woman who sweeps the house for a small coin of little worth. This reminds us that God's desire is always to include all that would otherwise be lost. Nothing is too slight, nothing too insignificant. Lost sheep, lost coin—and then, lost son.

The longest story of the chapter, the prodigal son parable, contains many rich motifs. But for our purposes, in the context of God's desire, the initial loss of the younger son is experienced by the father as the loss of some part of himself. It is part of the father that returns, to "complete" the father, and so he rejoices. The desire of the father is so powerful that it is in some sense the very presence of that desire that brings the boy to his senses in the pigsty. The same power drives the father down the road to draw the son home. In contrast, the elder brother cannot accept the returned sinner as brother; he can only speak of "this son of yours." The elder boy takes his stand on his consistent dutifulness. The problem is that a spirituality of duty rather than desire too easily results in self-righteousness. It also lacks love. We talk easily of a God of love. The writer of the First Letter of John goes further and says that God *is* love. But love is reciprocal. That is surely the inner life of God as implied by the doctrine of the Trinity—God as a mutuality of love. God's being is to love, but it is also to *be* loved. God is somehow incomplete if not loved.

Passionate or Passionless God?

These biblical allusions remind us once again that the images of God that predominate in both Hebrew and Christian scriptures are ones of passionate concern for creation. And yet a strong tradition grew up in early Christian theology—and continues to have influence today—that God was passionless. God's perfection is in the absence of passion. This makes it difficult for us to allow the reality of desire in God or its validity in our own spiritual quest. There have clearly been differences of approach to the question of passion and passionlessness. Sadly, the most pervasive in the longer term was the influence of late-Roman Stoic philosophy. Human passions were conceived of as diseases of the soul that were intrinsically evil. Theologians such as John Climacus could suggest that God could not be the creator of the passions! The virtue of *apatheia* in human beings, and as an inherent quality of God, then became not simply purity of heart or freedom from biased emotions leading to a vast openness to all creation but total passionlessness. Those in positions of leadership in the Christian community needed the same distance from the uncertainties of passion that God supposedly has. Leaders were to be in the image of a passionless God; detachment became the medium for revealing God. A classic expression of this approach to God appears in the first article of the Articles of Religion (or Thirty-Nine Articles) as they appear in the Anglican Book of Common Prayer: "There is but one living and true God, everlasting, without body, parts or passions."

A *Vulnerable God*

It seems that we desperately need to recover a sense of God who is not so much "power and might" as vulnerable. Jesus, the image of the unseen God,

> did not count equality with God
> something to be grasped.
> But he emptied himself,
> taking the form of a slave (Philippians 2:6-7).

If we accept that both the incarnation and the cross reveal the very heart of God, then we are bound to say that the nature of God is not to cling but to be self-emptying and to be nonpossessive. God continually risks a pouring out into the cosmos. For Julian of Norwich there is the continually repeated phrase, "in righteousness and in mercy he [God] wishes to be known and loved, now and forever" (*Showings*, chapter 35). God desires to relate to us because it is in God's very nature to do so. In the great mystical theology of the anonymous sixth-century writer Pseudo-Dionysius, which exercised such a powerful influence on the history of Christian spirituality, God is revealed in an outpouring into the cosmos and into human hearts of being, love and creativity. Yet, at the same time, God is beyond all attempts to describe or image. A spirituality that overemphasizes the last part of the equation, the unknowable quality of God, runs the risk of creating an essentially *protected* God. To insist, as the Christian tradition does, that God is ultimately beyond anything we can know has to be held in creative tension with the implication of our incarnational faith that the presence of God may be found in all human experiences—not least within human desire and intimacy.

Eros *in God*

The privileged image of God in the Christian tradition is Trinity. In this image God is essentially characterized in the most relational of categories, love. Equally, God-in-Trinity is dynamic rather than static because God is "being-in-relationship." It is important to express the inclusive nature of God's love and that God has no favorites in the notion of agape (or universal love). But we also need to redeem the notion of eros in God. God also loves specifically, longingly and in a particular way and this, essentially, is what eros love implies. Pseudo-Dionysius actually defines God as eros or longing:

> And we may be so bold as to claim ... that the Cause of all things loves all things in the superabundance of his goodness, that because of this goodness he makes all things, brings all things to perfection, holds all things together, returns all things. The divine longing [eros] is Good seeking good for the sake of the Good (*The Divine Names*, 4.10).

For Pseudo-Dionysius this divine longing causes God's movement out of self in an "ecstasy" of creation. God desires both to outpour and, at the same time, to draw all creation back into the divine life. So, ecstasy becomes reciprocal. God ecstatically goes out of self into the diversity of creation, including human beings. At the same time, each person is drawn out of fragmentation and dispersion into union, into the "singleness" of life in God. The power that describes both of these ecstasies is "eros."

To say that there is eros as well as agape in God expresses something important both about the love of God or human desire for God and about the erotic in human relations. As I have already hinted, we have inherited a distinction between agape love (disinterested or universal) and eros love (passionate and particular) that seems to make them two different kinds of love. A married Roman Catholic friend, in attempting to describe the difference between her spirituality and that of so many celibate clergy she knew, said jokingly, "The trouble with a husband and kids is that they attach you pretty firmly to *this* world." More graphically, she described sexual relations and child-rearing as "messy, sticky and smelly"! Is there any room for agape love in all this? It seems to me that this is a problem not merely for Roman Catholic spirituality but for so much of our Western spiritual heritage.

The problem is that the church tends to be uncomfortable with "the messy, sticky and smelly" quality that is an inherent part of every kind of human engagement. Our commitment to the particular, whether place or person, often struggles spiritually in a losing battle with what is presumed to be the higher value of detachment from all purely human loyalties. The Christian community is frequently tempted to retreat from real, down-to-earth human history into a condition of timelessness and into the myth of being perfect, self-contained and complete. An overbalanced spirituality of detachment or separation follows from a search for *reliability*. Because it tends to look toward a future, next-worldly completion, Christian spirituality sometimes appears to want nothing to do with what is perceived of as unreliable. Because flesh and human intimacy are affected by decay and uncertainty, they are patently not reliable. If what is sacred belongs to eternity, then what is connected with it should be imperishable. These equations and images of a detached God, associated only with agape love, tend to protect not only God but us from all that is impermanent.

Unity of Agape and Eros

A radical separation of agape love and eros love not only does not square with biblical images of God but also does not correspond to our human experience. It is possible to see agape, a more universal love, as something we always need to grow into rather than something we automatically possess. If we are honest, we inevitably experience our capacity to love initially as specific and exclusive. This can mean limited; human love is continually called to move beyond its instinctive limitations. There are those sharp reminders that God has no favorites (Acts 10:34 and Romans 2:11) and that "there can be neither Jew nor Greek, there can be neither slave nor free, there can be neither male nor female—for you are all one in Christ Jesus" (Galatians 3:28). However, truly disinterested love is not *impersonal*. It is deeply engaged and yet free from self-seeking. We can only learn how love may become disinterested agape in and through the grounded quality and passionate commitment of eros. We simply cannot bypass the call to committed, particular love in the search for self-transcending love. Agape and eros are not two different loves but two qualities in the one human love, just as they are complementary aspects of Love itself or God.

If we can recover the unity between agape and eros we may be able to resacralize the "erotic," which has too often been reduced to a superficial titillation of the senses. The relationship between the different forms of love should not be seen as opposition or choice. In the end, eros just as much as agape (*caritas*, "charity") is expressive of the same drive toward union with the One. Christianity's tendency to steer clear of the erotic has often set the spiritual over against human culture and experience. Spiritual passion for God has a close, positive relationship to other seemingly more ordinary forms of desire. In important respects the latter are doorways into the former. In other words, our relationship with God is expressed, "embodied" perhaps, in and through rather than despite all our human and material commitments.

Another danger in ignoring the spiritual significance of eros love is that this may actually undermine rather than enhance the possibility of a mystical experience of God. Combatting the anti-mystical tendencies of his own classical Protestant tradition, the Lutheran theologian Paul Tillich actually defines eros as "the mystical quality of love" (Tillich 1963). Religion without eros will tend to be reduced to moral values and dutiful rituals. A fixed cosmic order with no dynamism in God, merely an enforced faithfulness to the unchanging laws of divinity, means that stable social and religious roles will tend to outweigh the value of the great variety within our own personal lives. "If the eros quality of love with respect to God is rejected, the consequence of this rejection is that love toward God becomes an impossible concept ... replaced by mere obedience to God" (Tillich 1954, 30).

Eros in God also makes it possible to come to know the divine in the experience of human sexual relations. Indeed, human relations provide our primary image of God in everyday terms. It is not so much that God needs to be brought into human loving in order to redeem its essentially profane nature, but rather that true loving, true eroticism, is always an experience "in God." God *is* erotic power properly understood and is the erotic power between people. God is our capacity to love revealing itself in the matrix of all human relations. For Pseudo-Dionysius, God is both what all created reality yearns for and is also the very yearning itself as experienced in different ways at different levels of creation:

> Why is it ... that theologians sometimes refer to God as Yearning and Love and sometimes as the yearned-for and the Beloved? On the one hand he causes, produces, and generates what is being referred to, and, on the other hand, he is the thing itself (*The Divine Names*, 4.14).

As Paul Tillich put it more directly, "In every moment of genuine love we are dwelling in God and God in us" (Tillich 1954, 29).

Our desire, therefore, may be understood as a metaphor for embodying God. There is desire and an anguish of longing in us precisely because there is desire in God, in whose image we are created. Clearly, the desires that are significant for following the path of the gospel are those that, directly or indirectly, have to do with God. However, this does not necessarily imply a direct connection with personal prayer or worship. In principle, any event or set of circumstances may become a setting that stirs our deepest longings.

Christianity, founded on the belief of God's incarnation in the human person Jesus, exists to embody God. As a student in one of my courses powerfully suggested: "Our bodies are God's body language." This implies that what we do to and with our bodies, to other people's bodies and to all the embodiments that make up created reality, we do, as it were, to God.

Desire and the Spiritual Journey

Desire is also a metaphor for the journey into God as we are reminded by a medieval liturgical prayer, preserved as the well-known opening collect of the service of holy communion in the Anglican *Book of Common Prayer*:

> Almighty God, unto whom all hearts be open, all desires known, and from whom no secrets are hid: cleanse the thoughts of our hearts by the inspiration of thy Holy Spirit, that we may perfectly love thee, and worthily magnify thy holy name.

In the first eleven stanzas of the *Spiritual Canticle* of the sixteenth-century Spanish Carmelite John of the Cross, the human (and, we might say, cosmic) search for God is expressed in the symbol of the lover in search of the beloved:

> Why, since you wounded
> This heart, don't you heal it?
> And why, since you stole it from me,
> Do you leave it so,
> And fail to carry off what you have stolen?
> Extinguish these miseries,
> Since no one else can stamp them out;
> And may the vision of your beauty be my death;
> For the sickness of love
> Is not cured
> Except by your very presence and image(stanzas 9 and 10).

Spiritual longing is part of our identity as humans. Such longing urges us inward to our center at moments when the desires of the heart get entangled with the trivial. It also seems to me that the nature of longing, yearning and eros makes them more likely (as with the Spirit that blows where it will) to appear in our lives in forms that are challenging, unexpected and even prophetic rather than purely comforting and gratifying.

Another work of John of the Cross, *The Ascent of Mount Carmel* (Book 1, Chapter 2), speaks of the journey toward union with God in terms of a "dark night." As human beings, we are people of desire. At the center of our being is a deep longing that is painful because unsatisfied. Our loves in and for the world awaken desire and may, indeed, focus our experience of God. But if we remain only on the surface of these experiences they cannot bring fulfillment. The "dark night" cuts off human desires for a time and in the experience of emptiness sharpens desire and an awareness that ultimate fulfillment lies in union with God. The "dark night" is also experienced as an absence of an immediate sense of God. There is a close relationship here to the austere descriptions of the human quest for God in a modern American writer like Annie Dillard in her *Pilgrim at Tinker Creek*. For her, desire draws people to a spiritual North Pole, the harsh and furthest edge of the mystery. It also draws us up into "the gaps." "The gaps are the clefts in the rock where you cower to see the back parts of God." Desire drives us beyond the safe and manageable to "stalk the gaps" (Dillard 1977, 269).

A different way of evoking the connection between desire and absence is to be found in the beautifully expressed meditation on the appearance of the risen Jesus to Mary Magdalen (John 20:11-18) in one of the *Gospel Homilies* of Gregory the Great (whom some have called the Doctor of Desire). Desire has a dynamic quality because it is concerned with constant progress.

> We must stop and reflect upon the ardent love in the heart of this woman who would not leave the Lord's grave even after his own disciples had gone away. She continued seeking him whom she could not find; in tears she kept searching; and, afire with love, she

yearned for him whom she believed had been removed.... She had already sought and found nothing. But she persevered, and therefore found the object of her love. While she was seeking, her longing grew stronger and stronger until at highest pitch it was allayed in the embrace of him whom she was seeking. Holy desires grow with delay: if they fade through delay they are no desires at all (Feast of St Mary Magdalen, Roman Rite, July 22, Office of Readings).

The Song of Songs

To return to John of the Cross, much of his poetic language echoes that of the Song of Songs. This is not surprising, for it is the Song of Songs, the Hebrew scriptures' most direct use of erotic imagery, that found special favor with a range of spiritual writers from Origen to Bernard of Clairvaux, other medieval Cistercians, the Beguines and women mystics of all kinds. The Song of Songs is *the* scriptural text par excellence in Christian mystical writings. With these mystics, including the often complex writings of John of the Cross, a highly ascetic lifestyle and a sometimes convoluted theology were balanced by a sense of God that produced deep expressions of feeling in poetry and hymns. The mystics considered that the highly personalized language of the Song of Songs made it appropriate to describe God's relationship not merely with God's people, but also with individuals. The book's acceptance into the canon of Christian scripture, despite some theological misgivings, legitimized the presence of eros in the relationship between God and the human person.

The early church theologian Origen, for example, is quite insistent in using the word eros rather than the more respectable agape in his commentaries. And he effectively originated an extraordinary genre of Christian literature. The various commentaries and sermons—Origen and others—on the Song of Songs translate what, on the face of it, seem to be pretty human passions, poetically expressed, into quite

complex allegories of the believer's mystical search for union
with God the Beloved.

The Middle Ages in Western Europe particularly saw a
more general flowering of the language of love and marriage
in spiritual writings—and, indeed, of the quite explicit sexual
vocabulary of kisses and even intercourse. This use of sexual
language for the union with God was by no means confined to
women, even though the imagery for God remained
predominantly male. It depends very much on your point of
view whether this reflects an unhealthy repression of sexual
urges among celibate monastics and clergy that forced them to
come out in other ways, or whether it is a perfectly acceptable
process of harnessing the power of human desire toward its
origin and completion in God. My sense as a historian is that
the origin of this language reflects a peculiar mixture of the two.

As we shall see later, it is not at all clear in the Christian
tradition that the theological acceptance of eros in the divine-
human relationship, or the use of sexual language in mystical
writings, did much to legitimize the spiritual quality of the
erotic in human sexual relations. What the mystical tradition
undoubtedly does is to remind us of the powerful potential
of human desire in our relationship with God. This, in turn,
invites us to allow that relationship to move from a more
intellectual faith to connect with our deepest self. Here it can
be anchored in our natural powers and will engage our
emotional loyalties rather than remain on the surface of our
lives and actions.

Desire and Self-Image

Although our desire recognizes an absence and a lack,
and is therefore a dynamic movement toward what will fulfil
us, its liberation in us paradoxically depends on a healthy
sense of our own worth. We can only truly *desire* God, for
example, if we actually believe that we are capable of growth,
of movement toward a goal, toward a perfecting. The more
self-aware I am, in the best sense, the more I feel the pull of

this perfecting. My desire that some process of perfecting actually exists for me increases in proportion to the sense that my life is significant. So, desire for God is rooted in self-belief, which is why attention to our all too human desires, including their ambiguities, is not irrelevant but vital!

Indeed, the matter goes deeper than this. We need to discern, as we do in our human relationships, between the mature and the immature in the way we approach God. We need to learn the *human* "language" of desire and love. It is clearly possible to confuse a kind of saccharine-sweet piety for deep desire for God. But that, in religious terms, is the equivalent of mistaking skin-deep infatuation for mature love or a cheap romantic comic strip story for Shakespeare's *Romeo and Juliet*. Love costs, love hurts, love engages the whole of the self. Indeed, love, as a slowly unfolding process, involves a self-giving and self-transcendence that can only happen if there is already a healthy self-possession and a secure sense that self-gift will not become self-destruction. Only from such a secure place could we pray with Julian of Norwich:

> Our good Lord revealed that it is very greatly pleasing to him that a simple soul should come naked, openly and familiarly. For this is the loving yearning of the soul through the touch of the Holy Spirit, from the understanding which I have in this revelation: God, of your goodness give me yourself, for you are enough for me, and I can ask for nothing which is less which can pay you full worship. And if I ask anything which is less, always I am in want; but only in you do I have everything (*Showings*, chapter 5).

This brings us full circle back to God's desire and Eckhart's insight that God is free to desire and to let go of divine self-containment in creating, loving and redeeming because in God there is no ultimate loss of self in doing so. God's way of loving does not diminish God but reaches out to be inclusive of all true loves. The nature of God's loving desire and our love of God do not in any way contradict our other human loves. On the contrary. The divine dimension in ourselves simply enables all our loves to be experienced in their full reality. Progress in praying, as opposed to mere improvement in prayer technique, consists in coming ever closer to that dimension in us that is open to love and which can receive from moment to moment the gift of existence in God's activity of creating. This human capacity for love is generative *at the same time* of human commitments and openness to the divine presence.

So I was taught that love is our Lord's meaning. And I saw very certainly in this and in everything, that before God made us he loved us, which love was never abated and never will be. And in this love he has done all his works, and in this love he has made all things profitable to us, and in this love our life is everlasting. In our creation we had beginning, but the love in which he created us was in him from without beginning. In this love we have our beginning, and all this shall we see in God without end (*Showings*, chapter 86).

THREE

Desire and Prayer

It is for these reasons sometimes that these tears flow
and desires come, and they are furthered by human
nature and one's temperament; but finally ... they
end in God regardless of their nature (Teresa of Avila,
The Interior Castle, Fourth Mansion, chapter 1.6).

During my adolescent years, when the faith of my family
background was slowly translating itself into a personal
commitment, my relationship with God and my prayer was
full of feeling. Much of it was undoubtedly naive and some
of it was superficial. But I had no doubts that feelings had a
proper place in prayer. My image of God, as far as I can recall
it, was one that enabled me to express myself quite freely.

Unfortunately, when I entered a religious community
direct from school in my late teens, the kind of prayer we
were exposed to was vastly different. Feelings were definite-
ly suspect. Warnings about the danger of reading contemplative writers was not simply a safeguard against adolescent
extremism but also accorded with a sense that our kind of
prayer (unless it was devotional piety of a traditional kind)
should use the mind and will rather than the heart. It does
not seem to me to be a coincidence, as I look back, that my
overall relationship with God became less relaxed and less

trusting. It took years of wise spiritual direction later on to repair the damage.

In her discussion of meditation, some of which I quote at the beginning of this chapter, Teresa of Avila makes a clear distinction between feelings or "consolations" and "spiritual delights." The first seem to be related explicitly to the human activity of prayer. The latter cannot in any sense be acquired and come in some direct way from God. However, the point that it seems important to emphasize is that for Teresa, as for other great teachers of prayer, human desires, passions and love are not only valid but have a central role to play. "I only wish to inform you that in order to profit by this path and ascend to the dwelling places we desire, the important thing is not to think much but to love much; and so do that which best stirs you to love" (Fourth Mansion, chapter 1.7). Attending to our desires as we relate to God in prayer grounds us firmly in our bodies, our identities and the world in which we find ourselves. It is through all these things that the divine Spirit offers us a union with God. "Finally ... they end in God regardless of their nature."

True Prayer

It seems fair to say that our human experience is a paradoxical mixture of, on the one hand, connectedness and harmony with other people and the world around us and, on the other, disharmony and estrangement. The good connections are made and the possible healing of any estrangement gradually brought about through particular transformative experiences within our everyday existence. These may or may not be self-consciously "spiritual." However, this is prayer in the broadest sense. Prayer is, therefore, not just one activity among others—explicitly and exclusively focused on God—but the whole rich mixture of event, action and receiving gifts that constitutes our relationship with God in the midst of human life. For the Lutheran theologian Paul Tillich, whether it was in sexual love, moments of true insight or the appreciation of art, nature and other people, "contemplation means going into the temple, the sphere of the holy, into the deep roots of things, into their creative ground." In human beings and in nature "we see the mysterious power we call beauty and truth and goodness." We see God "with and through the shape of a rose and the movements of the stars and the image of a friend" (Tillich 1955, 30).

True prayer is a matter both of the heart and the head. It is a unity of love and knowledge, and its dynamism is our desire. There is a tendency to think of knowledge only in terms of objective analysis. Paul Tillich not only sought to rescue religious "knowledge" from such a limited definition but sought to explore a fundamental unity among it, the ecstasy of mysticism and the desire of human love. "Love includes the knowledge of the beloved. But it is not the knowledge of analysis and calculating manipulation." It is "participating knowledge which changes both the knower and the known in the very act of knowledge" (Tillich 1963, 137). "Participating knowledge" is a reasonably good description of desire in relation to prayer. For as that great teacher of spiritual desire, Ignatius Loyola, reminds us, "what fills and satisfies the soul consists, not in knowing much, but in our understanding the realities profoundly and savoring them interiorly" (*Spiritual Exercises*, no. 2). Participating knowledge is what matters. Attending to desire, both our own and, through it, God's desiring in us, is the way to the kind of knowledge that can transform our lives.

As I have already suggested, desire is a metaphor for the whole process of journeying into God. In this journey we both learn how to embody God and, at the same time, recognize the need to transcend the limitations of our images of God. Desire is, as we shall see later, also a metaphor for choosing from within ourselves rather than from outside. Prayer as relationship is a continual experience of confronting choice. In the mind of Ignatius Loyola, for example, we grow into the fullness of being human in the process of choosing—which is why the where and the how of our choosing is so vital. Because attention to desire may lead us to touch our "essential self," it enables us to discern which of our choices are most expressive of who we truly are. And in the same process, desire becomes a metaphor of transformation—of being gradually freed from all that encumbers us and stops us growing or moving onward.

We may seek to fill our emptiness with more and more experiences just as we accumulate material possessions. Yet, I would suggest that a realization of true desire is in fact God within, gifting us with a necessary dissatisfaction with anything less than everything! And that everything is not the same as the accumulation of things.

> You ... live not by your natural inclinations, but by the Spirit, since the Spirit of God has made a home in you.

> All who are guided by the Spirit of God are [children] of God; for what you received was not the spirit of slavery to bring you back into fear; you received the Spirit of adoption, enabling us to cry out, "*Abba*, Father." The Spirit...joins with our spirit to bear witness that we are children of God.

> When we do not know how to pray properly, then the Spirit personally makes our petitions for us in groans that cannot be put into words. And the God who can see into all hearts knows what the Spirit means because the prayers that the Spirit makes for God's holy people are always in accordance with the mind of God (Romans 8:9, 14-16, 26-27).

Desire Is Prayer

True desire is non-possessive. It is an openness to future, to possibility, to the other—whether a human other or God. This is true of sexual desire too, if it is not simply infatuation. Desire is as much about self-giving as about wishing to receive. That is why desire is such a wonderful metaphor for prayer. Or perhaps desire *is* prayer, if we recall that moving phrase of Tillich, "In every moment of genuine love we are dwelling in God and God in us." In every moment of deep desire we are in God. To know God and to know the depths of ourselves is ultimately the same thing. "And I saw very certainly that we must necessarily be in longing and in penance until the time when we are led so deeply into God that we verily and truly know our own soul" (Julian, *Showings*, chapter 56). As non-possessive, our deep desire has no limit (for it touches infinity) and equally does not seek to limit what it reaches out toward.

The way of true desire is a way of attentive, contemplative awareness of ourselves, other people and the world around—and, in all of them, God. As such, it is not just a self-indulgent journey inward but is simultaneously a movement outward. Contemplative prayer and action do not oppose each other. Rather, each is the precondition of the other. The way of desire, therefore, also seeks the transformation of our relationships—from a tendency to be self-serving to being increasingly non-possessive, non-oppressive, non-hierarchical. To allow ourselves to touch deep desire is to open ourselves to being purged of thoughtless and self-centered wanting. This is profoundly challenging to all our ways of seeking to define others in terms of ourselves or our group. That is why truly contemplative people touch, with compassion and with pain, the heart of their own self, the edge of infinity and equally all reality around them. That is why the way of desire is also a way of conversion and transformation.

To live in the heart of true desire, and to pray from that heart, is a powerful thing. If only we could reach that point more consistently! "I tell you, therefore, everything you ask and pray for, believe that you have it already, and it will be yours" (Mark 11:24). Julian of Norwich talks of the prayer of beseeching as founded on God, even given to us by God. And in that beseeching lies a union between our will and God's.

"Beseeching is a true and gracious, enduring will of the soul, united and joined to our Lord's will by the sweet, secret operation of the Holy Spirit" (*Showings*, chapter 41).

It is recorded that Mother Teresa of Calcutta said that when she first started her homes for the destitute the sisters sometimes lacked the necessary money or other resources to carry on. Yet a period of intense prayer always seemed to produce the necessary results. We should not think that it has anything to do with the sheer quantity of prayer or even its emotional intensity. It is not simply because we want very strongly that we receive. The mystery of petitionary prayer cannot be solved so cheaply. What it does point to, however, is that the degree to which we pray in harmony with our deepest desires, in congruence with our truest self, and open to God desiring in us, governs the harmony that will exist between our asking and what is appropriately given.

In a sense, *true* desire is all. If we are truly focused—what Buddhists call single pointed—and desire something single-heartedly out of the depths of ourselves, it can be ours. Praying for something authentically means to want it with every fiber of our being rather than partially or ambivalently. We often fall short, perhaps in not deciding what we most truly want or, again, not daring to admit that we want anything at all. The reason may be that we fear selfishness. But it may also be that to desire something strongly enough is always to deprive ourself of the alternatives. To harness our energies to one profound desire is to make a decision. To decide is to choose and exclude and thus to experience a small death. Yet the experience of many people is that if it is authentic it will be a moment of enlightenment and expansion rather than of fundamental loss. The deep desire we hardly perceived breaks through the wants that we are able to see, and around which we made our conscious choice, and is immediately recognizable as the only thing we ever really wanted.

Desire and Ignatius Loyola

So, I believe that desire and contemplation are intimately connected. As the great Franciscan mystical theologian Bonaventure reminds us, "No one is in anyway disposed for divine contemplation that leads to mystical ecstasy unless ... he is a man of desires" (*The Soul's Journey into God*, Prologue, 3). One of the most striking practical exponents of desire as the way to dispose ourselves for contemplation and service was Ignatius Loyola. As we have already seen, he suggests that a vital prelude at the beginning of every period of prayer "is to ask God our Lord for what I want and desire" (*Spiritual Exercises*, no. 48). In the context of the process of making the Exercises, this undoubtedly serves to highlight the main focus of each part of the retreat—its mood, so to speak. However, the effect is to center the whole experience of prayer on desire in such a way that we could say that desire, understood as an increasing openness to God's possibilities for us, is the essence of our prayer whatever structure or method we adopt. This too is at least one aspect of the statement in *The Cloud of Unknowing* that "now you are to stand in desire, all your life long, if you are to make progress in the way of perfection" (chapter 2).

To ask for what I desire, or to stand in desire is likely to be an experience of conversion and change. If desire, our longing, is to be truly liberated, we must learn to want what can actually answer our longing. We need to discover, slowly perhaps, that what we long for is "the All," the infinite, rather than simply everything as the sum total of what we can accumulate, grasp or control by our own means. When Ignatius Loyola suggests that we ask God for what we desire, this may also, on one level, be a request that we come to know what it really is that we desire or need to desire. It may also be a request to be free enough to ask truly for our deepest desire although we have to admit that at this point we do not want it wholeheartedly!

It is very important to grasp that when spiritual teachers such as Ignatius Loyola talk about desire they do not mean that we should artificially "crank ourselves up." We are not expected to ask for some "appropriate" desire or spiritual sentiment, whatever we actually feel. This would be dishonest and ultimately destructive. Ignatius Loyola suggests as another prelude to prayer "a composition made by imagining the place" (*Spiritual Exercises*, no. 47). Commentators over the years have used a great deal of ink arguing about what this means! But at the very least it involves gathering things together in order to be properly prepared for prayer. We are at the heart of this gathering together as we are. So, it is possible to say that the process is one of composing ourselves, or situating ourselves, in the spiritual and psychological "place" where we are. In the face of God, this "place" certainly involves the truth of the particular moment. Yet the "place" is also always provisional. Thus, if we link this to asking for what we desire, it is possible to see that prayer involves seeking to place ourselves in a space before God that is honest and also seeking to be open to change. Then, to ask for what we desire may become an openness to what God desires for us and in us at this moment, in this place in which we are composed and waiting. This openness to God is inevitably only partial at any given moment. But it invites God at least to touch our center, where the deepest desires dwell in order to unlock their power and potential.

Before passing on, three final remarks can be made about desire in the mind of Ignatius Loyola. First, desires in particular moments of prayer are not totally discrete things but relate to each other to reveal, ever more fully, the pattern of our relationship with God. So, it is vital to discover the thread that links our desires together. We might say that we need to recognize the deep desire behind the desires we more easily express. This process of contemplative awareness of self takes great patience and requires moments of reflective stillness. We are influenced by so many expectations, pat-

terns of conventional thinking and behavior, as well as fears
of change, that deciding what we truly want (or, which of the
many wants is most true!) is not a simple matter.

I wonder how many of us know what pleasing ourselves really means. The trouble is that people who "please
themselves" are said to be selfish or irresponsible. That immediately preempts any possibility of discovering what truly
pleases the self. And yet we are asked to love our neighbor
as ourselves. Do we know who that self really is and what
loving it would look like? In extreme situations Ignatius
Loyola was not beyond letting some confused young Jesuits
be, in conventional terms, thoroughly irresponsible for a
time. He believed that if they had the freedom to do exactly
what they felt like, rather than what was expected, they might
become aware more freely of what they deeply *wanted*! Yet, in
practice, I suspect that many of us would find it hard to take
that degree of risk with ourselves, let alone with other people.

Second, our deepest desires need to be stimulated. A
powerful medium for this is our imagination. Again, when
Ignatius Loyola talks about "composition of place" in prayer,
the phrase he actually uses is "a composition made by seeing
[or imagining] the place." In the context of the Exercises,
Ignatius suggests particular desires that seem appropriate to
the mood of the retreat process. As I have already suggested,
these should not be understood as "oughts" or as an invitation to dishonest sentiments. An alternative perspective is to
let the suggestions act as a stimulus to our imagination
regarding *possibilities* beyond the immediately obvious or
even manageable. As a more general principle, it seems good
to expand the desires we choose to name so that they might
tap into our deeper longings and upgrade our hopes as to
what God might give.

I wonder whether this understanding of Ignatius
Loyola's way of proceeding may even throw a different light
on how some of Jesus' enigmatic sayings about prayer and
faith are intended to operate? "Ask, and it will be given to
you; search, and you will find; knock, and the door will be

opened to you" (Matthew 7:7). "In truth I tell you if your faith is the size of a mustard seed you will say to this mountain, 'Move from here to there,' and it will move; nothing will be impossible for you" (Matthew 17:20). I have been particularly struck by one final saying in reference to providence: "Set your hearts his kingdom first, and on God's saving justice, and all these other things will be given you as well" (Matthew 6:33). Desire *big* things, the biggest of all that God can give, the coming of the Kingdom, and you will find that the smaller needs are not rejected but always included in that gift.

Third, we can expect conflicts between apparently opposing desires to be the general rule rather than the exception. We will return to this in more detail when we consider the relationship between desires and making choices. In fact, Ignatius's wisdom was that we should be worried if there were no conflicts (*Spiritual Exercises*, no. 6). Why should this be important? First, the chances are that a complete absence of inner conflict in our lives indicates a lack of emotional engagement rather than deep peace. But, more than this, the greater our sensitivity to our authentic, deep desires, the more aware we will become of the tension between these and the temptations to counterfeit behavior that all of us experience daily.

Desire and Julian

If we can say that for Ignatius Loyola desire *is* prayer, it is also fair to suggest that for Julian of Norwich one of the essential dimensions of prayer is longing. Julian's main teaching on prayer lies in her Revelation XIV, which runs from chapter 41 to chapter 63 of the so-called Long Text of her *Showings* (or *Revelations of Divine Love*, as they are sometimes called). For Julian, longing and beseeching are indications of God working within us.

And our Lord ... said: "I am the ground of your beseeching. First, it is my will that you should have

it, and then I make you to wish it, and then I make
you to beseech it."

For everything which our good Lord makes us to
beseech he himself has ordained for us from all eternity. So here we may see that our beseeching is not
the cause of the goodness and grace which he gives
us, but his own goodness (chapter 41).

Julian's treatment of desire, or longing, in relationship
to prayer is more comprehensive, basic and dynamic than
many other spiritual writers. Her understanding of desire
seems to have expanded in the course of her experiences, and
so she shares with us her perceptions of what and how we
are to desire in order to become one with God. For Julian, our
deepest natural desire is to have nothing less than God.

For this is the loving yearning of the soul through the
touch of the Holy Spirit, from the understanding
which I have in this revelation: God, of your goodness
give me yourself, for you are enough for me, and I
can ask for nothing which is less which can pay you
full worship. And if I ask anything which is less,
always I am in want; but only in you do I have
everything (chapter 5).

This desire is so great that we would not be content
without God even if we had all other things.

The natural desire of our soul is so great and so
immeasurable that if all the nobility which God ever
created in heaven and on earth were given to us for
our joy and our comfort, if we did not see his own fair
blessed face, still we should never cease to mourn and
to weep in the spirit (chapter 72).

"For [God] wants us to know that in a short time we
shall see clearly in him all that we desire." For Julian, it was
not knowledge but desire itself, and its strength, that really
counted. "Still it seemed to me humble and petty in com-

parison with the great desire which the soul has to see God" (chapter 47).

The unlocking of our desire in prayer creates a dynamic whereby the least encounter with God stirs us to seek more. The more we experience the reality of God, the more we desire God.

> When we by his special grace behold him plainly, seeing no other, we then necessarily follow him, and he draws us to him by love. For I saw and felt that his wonderful and total goodness fulfills all our powers; and with that I saw that his continual working in every kind of thing is done so divinely, so wisely and so powerfully that it surpasses all our imagining and everything we can understand or think. And then we can do no more than contemplate him and rejoice, with a great and compelling desire to be wholly united into him, and attend to his motion and rejoice in his love and delight in his goodness (chapter 43).

But this dynamic has a perpetual quality of incompleteness, for we never come to *possess* God finally. "So I saw him and sought him, and I had him and lacked him" (chapter 10). Desire is, therefore, a permanent part of our lives—the condition of openness to God's reality as it unfolds infinitely and eternally.

Desire and Hadewijch

The fact that our deepest desire is never definitively satisfied is also a painful matter. Julian's "I had him and I lacked him" has a very poignant feel to it. So does the love-mysticism of the thirteenth-century Flemish beguine Hadewijch, who in her visions experienced Christ speaking to her of "painful desire" and the "privation of what you desire above all ... this reaching out to me who am unreachable" (*The Complete Works*, 283). Hadewijch has a great deal more to say about the unquiet nature of desire in one of her poems in couplets (no. 10), "Not Feeling but Love." In our "childish" love we sometimes want to be satisfied with "many particular things," because we mistake the "delight" of good feelings for true "desire." In Hadewijch's experience, this would be to settle for substantially less than we are called to.

> Not for feeling's sake must we learn to serve,
> But only to love with love in Love.

The difference between delight and desire offers an interesting comparison with what Ignatius Loyola teaches about spiritual consolation in his "Rules for the Discernment of Spirit" (*Spiritual Exercises,* nos. 313-36). Consolation should not be mistaken for pleasurable or good feelings—although these may be part of the experience at times. Consolation is an experience of being drawn toward what is life-giving, toward inner freedom, toward real love, ultimately toward God. It is fairly obvious from our common experience that all these things may actually be quite painful and certainly challenging. Ignatius recognizes this clearly. And yet there is an underlying sense of rightness, peace and harmony that actually enables us to move on even in the midst of surface difficulties. This is "a peace which the world cannot give" (John 14:27). Although, on the face of it, his dry prose lacks the evocative qualities of a Hadewijch, Ignatius tries to express a paradoxical quality in "consolation" similar to that present in her more poetic descriptions of "desire."

For Hadewijch, in order to reach the unreachable God who is Love, we need to love without rest and "desire above measure"—that is, beyond reason and thought. So our spirit, even

> when it feels misery,
> It can learn to know Love's mode of action.

The effect of divine Love in us is that,

> The proximity of the nature of Love
> Deprives the soul of its rest:
> The more Love comes, the more she steals.

To those who really seek to live, riskily, in Love and who enter what Hadewijch calls the divine "abyss," Love "gives an unquiet life." Why? Because divine Love "causes hearts, in Love, to be in constant striving."

> Desires of love, moreover, cannot
> By all these explanations be quieted.
> Desire strives in all things for more than it possesses:
> Love does not allow it to have any rest.

In a daring and controversial statement (also present in her Letter 8 and Vision 13), Hadewijch suggests that a "noble unfaith" is higher than "fidelity." While fidelity is related to reason and "often lets desire be satisfied," unfaith "never allows desire any rest in any fidelity." This unfaith, which is expressed as a negative quality, is difficult to define but perhaps is also best approached negatively! It consists of living in the absence of consoling feelings. It is the opposite of peaceful rest, which settles for less than the All. It turns our spirit away from taking pleasure "in what it has in hand." It is suspicious of divine Love in the sense of anything that can be grasped. Thus, at the heart even of Hadewijch's rich spirituality of love the total otherness of God is somehow expressed.

There appear to be similarities here to the more austere mysticism of "unknowing" present, for example, in Meister Eckhart's paradoxical teaching that Christians should be so poor that they do not even have God, or in the writings of the contemporary Welsh priest-poet R. S. Thomas.

> Why no! I never thought other than
> That God is that great absence
> In our lives, the empty silence

Within, the place where we go
Seeking, not in hope to
Arrive or find (Thomas 1984, "Via Negativa")

The moment you feel yourself to be in definitive contact with the reality of God, you have missed God. Hadewijch's unfaith bypasses what is manageable and controllable in human terms. "Love hurts," as the title of a recent British television romantic soap reminds us! There is a painful quality to all true love, because love is ultimately there for the sake of love not for feelings of security or satisfaction. If we have ever found ourselves continuing to love "beyond the immediate facts" in our relationship with another person we will have a small inkling of what Hadewijch understands about our relationship with God.

Active Desire

If desire in prayer is unlocked, there is another dynamic present that consists of a gradual movement toward not only our own deepest desire but also, in and through that, toward God's own desiring within us. As Julian suggests,

> For the whole reason why we pray is to be united into the vision and contemplation of him to whom we pray, wonderfully rejoicing with reverent fear, and with so much sweetness and delight in him that we cannot pray at all except as he moves us at the time.

> And so I saw that when we see the need for us to pray, then our Lord God is following us, helping our desire (*Showings*, chapter 43).

In other words, God is the one who places desire in our hearts and who is the completion of all true desires. "I am he who makes you to long; I am he, the endless fulfilling of all true desires" (*Showings*, chapter 59). It is not that to desire God is the only valid desire, with other, more physical or material desires as mere distractions. It is not a matter of choosing between God and other loves or needs. Julian was quite explicit that she wrote about her mystical experiences for the benefit of all Christians without exception, whatever their lifestyle. Although she had chosen a solitary life at some point in her adulthood, she clearly did not believe that it was the only life compatible with contemplative mysticism. It would be better to say that Julian taught that if our desires, whatever they are, are true to our deepest self they are God-filled.

For Julian, as for many mystics, desire is not entirely passive—some kind of lingering longing. It is active, and it is powerful. Even in the more passive, mystical Sixth Mansion of her *Interior Castle*, Teresa of Avila writes of the soul being brought to desire God "vehemently." And throughout *The Cloud of Unknowing* the author links desire, or its equivalents, to such active verbs as *labor*: "You are to smite upon that thick cloud of unknowing with a sharp dart of longing love" (chapter 6). Desire often involves what we might call an intentional longing or focused longing for God. That seems to be an especially good description of what Ignatius Loyola implies when he suggests that we *ask* for what we desire. But it is also part of the teaching on contemplation in *The Cloud of Unknowing*. There, the language of stripping ourselves of every thought and desire for what is not God does not imply the *destruction* of human desire but its intense concentration, which can fan a spark into a flame. For, if directed toward many objects separately, our desire is dissipated. The aim of contemplation is to unite all our desires toward one object in concentrated intensity.

Is our state of desire, our focused longing, a permanent condition? Surely once we are united with God our desire is fulfilled. Well, in one sense we are from the start united with God, who is unchangeable goodness. This is the precondition of our journeying, not merely the final conclusion. "For our soul is so wholly united to God, through his own goodness, that between God and our soul nothing can interpose" (*Showings*, chapter 46). Yet it is this very union with God that deepens desire. Material needs may be satisfied, but that is never so of the desire for the infinite. Rather, the paradox is that as God's presence is perceived more deeply so desire is increased rather than satisfied. For Julian, God is a God of desire and this quality in God lasts until the end of time.

> Which desire, longing and thirst, as I see it, were in him from without beginning; and he will have this until the time that the last soul which will be saved has come up into his bliss (chapter 31).

Whether we can understand desire as existing even beyond this, in whatever we mean by eternal life, is something to which we will return later.

So, it would appear that longing and desire, ours and God's, are qualities that remain until we are caught into God's "bliss." We never possess God or encompass the infinite. For us in relation to God there will always be the promise of more, because we cannot experience any limit to what it is we ultimately desire. As one of the great spiritual teachers of the Eastern church, Gregory of Nyssa, reminds us, communion with God is an experience of continual expansion. In meeting God we can never be filled in an ultimate sense. Desire as openness to possibility and to love ever remains in us. "This truly is the vision of God: never to be satisfied in the desire to see him. But one must always, by looking at what he can see, rekindle his desire to see more" (*The Life of Moses*, Book 2, 239).

FOUR

Desire and Sexuality

Where, like a pillow on a bed,
A Pregnant banke swel'd up, to rest
The violets reclining head,
Sat we two, one anothers best.
Our hands were firmely cimented
With a fast balme, which thence did spring,
Our eye-beames twisted, and did thred

Our eyes, upon one double string....
This Extasie doth unperplex
(We said) and tell us what we love,
Wee see by this, it was not sexe,
Wee see, we saw not what did move:
But as all severall soules containe
Mixture of things, they know not what,
Love, these mixt soules doth mixe againe,
And makes both one, each this and that....

But O alas, so long, so farre
Our bodies why doe wee forbeare?
They'are ours, though they'are not wee, Wee are
The intelligences, they the spheare.
We owe them thankes, because they thus,
Did us, to us, at first convey,
Yeelded their forces, sense, to us,
Nor are drosse to us, but allay.

On man heavens influence workes not so,
But that it first imprints the ayre,
Soe soule into the soule may flow,
Though it to body first repaire....

To'our bodies turne wee then, that so
Weake men on love reveal'd may looke;
Loves mysteries in soules doe grow,
But yet the body is his booke
(From John Donne, "The Extasie").

Some years ago I was accompanying an older married man during his retreat. In his prayer he had been focusing on the image of the potter in the opening verses of Jeremiah, chapter 18. "Yes, like clay in the potter's hand, so you are in mine, House of Israel." As he identified himself with the clay, the man found to his surprise that the thought of God's hands shaping him, especially re-forming him, was very frightening. We agreed that he should return to the same scripture passage in the course of the next day's prayer to see whether there would be any further enlightenment. Although it was unplanned and not his usual form of prayer, the man found himself visualizing the hands of God reaching out toward him. He tried honestly to invite God to shape him. But he could not do so; the experience still felt too threatening. As he described it to me during our conversation the next day, he eventually gave up the struggle and simply sat blankly with himself, his fears and God. Quite unexpectedly the image of hands reaching out toward him returned. However, before he could once again recoil in fear, he saw that God's hands were the hands of his wife, which had caressed him so many times during their long marriage. It was a profound conversion experience on several levels.

Clearly, something important about the man's fearful images of God was made explicit and healed in a substantial way. The man also took a step forward in the process of lowering his instinctive defenses and letting go in trust.

However, most striking of all, the man understood that God's touch had been at the heart of all his human love and sexual intimacy.

The Christian mystical tradition has often used the language of sexual love and eroticism both in terms of God's way of relating to humanity and our way of union with God. However, this has usually implied the *transformation* of the sexual energy of eros into distinctively spiritual channels. The trouble is that, from quite an early stage of its history, Christianity also has tended to treat sexuality and "the erotic" as particularly symptomatic of a world fallen away from God. Thus sexual ecstasy is never to be compared with spiritual ecstasy and consequently is unable to contribute to our relationship with God. Usually, sexual feelings are considered a profound problem! At an ecumenical workshop on human sexuality, a number of people commented that some members of their churches still thought of sex as a necessary evil and not as a gift of God to be enjoyed. For classical Christianity it was human sexual *language* that was usable in terms of human encounters with God, not human sexual *experience*. The result was an uncomfortable paradox. While eros transformed into spiritual energy might be fine, there had to be, at the same time, a complete separation between holiness and sexuality.

Every human person is unavoidably a sexual being. This emphatically includes those in various forms of singleness, including the option for celibacy. We can try to ignore sexuality and to repress it, or we can seek to live positively and healthily within it. What is not open to us is to bypass it or to escape completely from it.

The historical origins of Christianity's traditional problems with the body, passion and sexuality are complex. Perhaps the most elegantly written, comprehensive and balanced account in English is Peter Brown's *The Body and Society*, which charts the rise of sexual renunciation in early Christianity. Many factors played their part. There was, first of all, a certain inheritance from Stoic philosophy. Here, spiritual significance was accorded to the repudiation of pleasure and to the avoidance of uncontrolled passion. Then there were late imperial Roman attitudes to masculinity as the measure of what it was to be human. This involved the need to maintain male "integrity" by means of detachment, self-sufficiency, autonomy and avoidance of softness. These cultural values were reinforced by the theological link that was gradually forged between the wholeness, involving resurrection of the body, that was our presumed destiny in heaven and the desire to anticipate this through the bodily intactness of virginity in the here and now.

The result was that for much of the Christian era the perceived precondition of a profound spirituality has been the absence of active sexuality. If this was not precisely perpetual virginity, then widowhood or some kind of voluntary sexual abstinence would do. For example, the medieval English mystic Margery Kempe was a married woman who was reassured in visions that God also loved married people! Yet once she had experienced her first vision of heavenly bliss she wrote that she had no further sexual desire for her husband and even came to think of sexual relations as abominable. She eventually persuaded her husband to join with her in a mutual vow of chastity (*The Book of Margery Kempe*, Book 1, chapters 3-10). True, in Margery's historical context of extremely unequal relations between the sexes, chastity could be a form of social, sexual and spiritual liberation for her and other medieval women mystics. But the issue is obviously more complex because Margery, for example, was prepared to testify that sexual relations with her husband had in fact once been "a great delight" to both of them.

Obviously, we cannot entirely bypass these difficulties that we have inherited about linking spirituality and sexuality. However, we want to concentrate here on exploring positive ways of re-envisioning human sexuality, including its active expression, as a path to holiness and to God. This chapter begins with selected quotations from the poem "The Extasie" by the late sixteenth-century poet John Donne.

Most commentators traditionally distinguish between his "divine" poems and his "secular" ones. The latter are frequently concerned with human love and sometimes charged with sexual imagery. Yet Donne the human lover was also Dean Donne of St. Paul's Cathedral, London, an Anglican priest who also had strong Roman Catholic family roots.

For Donne there was no radical gulf between grace and nature, between the spiritual and the bodily. His vision of the human person, most famously expressed in his poetic line, "No man is an island, apart from the main," is one of connection rather than autonomy. The whole of the natural world is graced, and consequently so is sexual experience. John Donne almost certainly drew upon his Catholic roots, not least the spirituality of the mystics and of his contemporary, St. Francis de Sales, as well as on his own experience of love and marriage, to bring out the sacred (and, on occasion, mystical) quality of sexual love. It seems that his was one of the earliest explicit attempts in mainstream Western Christianity to appreciate sexual love as, at least potentially, spiritual experience.

Even if the greater part of the Western mystical tradition has not tended to consider direct sexual experience respectable in terms of our encounter with God, it remains a fact that writers such as Teresa of Avila at least found in sexual ecstasy the most adequate analogy to spiritual ecstasy. This leaves us with something that we can build upon. I suggest that the special quality the mystics found in the language of human sexuality implicitly supports that human loving is a shape taken by the love of God.

In trying to sketch out the beginnings of a spirituality of sexual desire, we will focus on five themes. First, although we opened up the question of eros and the erotic in Chapter 1, we need to look at some further aspects of what we understand by them. Second, we can assert that a conscious and healthy sexuality is not necessarily genitally active. There is no well-developed spirituality of singleness in terms of sexuality. If spirituality in the churches has been explicitly linked to sexuality at all, it has been limited to conventional marriage and the birth of children. As one ordinand recently said to me, the most commonly used rituals provided by all the mainline churches are baptism, marriage and funerals. Only the latter includes single people! Therefore, it is important to look at the question of human intimacy in the broadest sense. A great deal of what may be said about sexual union may also be said of non-genital intimacy, although the sexual union of two deeply committed people certainly focuses and enables certain spiritual experiences in a particularly powerful way. Whether we live sexually active lives or not, a balance between solitude and intimacy is an important psychological and spiritual need for all of us. Third, turning explicitly to active sexual relations, we will consider the experience of sexual union as a form of liberation from the tyranny of private will. Fourth, we will look again at possible connections between sexual ecstasy and union with God. Finally, we will reflect on the difference between abusive or invasive relationships and the respectful crossing of personal boundaries that is involved in healthy sexual intimacy.

The Erotic

Sadly, when a Christian like me starts writing about the spiritual qualities of the erotic or, more directly, about sex as a holy act, it can end up sounding rather like the more eccentric utterings of the Bhagwan Rajneesh! This is extremely unfortunate and has a great deal to do with the kind of sexual reductionism that pervades Western thinking these days. It is a pity that Christianity has not found a way (perhaps because it has not been sufficiently interested) to reinterpret, in inspirational modern guise, the patriarchal assumptions of the Letter to the Ephesians. There is, nonetheless, a great deal of potential in the epistle's quasi-mystical understanding of married sexual union.

Husbands must love their wives as they love their own bodies; for a man to love his wife is for him to love himself. A man never hates his own body, but he feeds it and looks after it; and that is the way Christ treats the Church, because we are parts of his Body. This is why a man leaves his father and mother and becomes attached to his wife, and the two become one flesh. This mystery has great significance but I am applying it to Christ and the Church (Ephesians 5:28-32).

Aspects of this would also be applicable to deeply intimate but not genital friendships between single people whose sexuality is mature. Eros love does transcend purely physical desire, but it does not bypass it. When directed toward another human being, eros love includes the physical but is not oriented *primarily or exclusively* to pleasure or to the release of physical tension. Eros love strives ultimately for union with whatever we perceive to be the source of all value for us. Or, as the eminent American psychologist Rollo May suggests, eros is "the drive toward union with what we belong to." Toward harmony and unity and integrity and meaning. In Christian terms this is not some impersonal force but is God-in-me, God-in-the-other and God-as-the-love-between-us. This move toward union involves a process of transcending our sense of fragmentation and separation. In an alienated or dysfunctional culture, eros love actually may be in conflict with the prevailing misshapen attitudes to "sex." A true eros love views "the other," our partner, as a subject with which we seek to be united rather than an object to be used for pleasure, release or breeding.

There is an important difference between false eroticism and true eros love. The first is an uncontrolled desire to draw other people into ourself. It therefore tends to be invasive and possessive. If we are prone to false eroticism, ultimately we want to be gratified. We do not truly want other people for themselves. In contrast, eros love is a unitive power bringing together elements that belong to each other. The crucial thing is that desire is not purely instinctual. In terms of human sexual encounter, true desire is always a desire for another person mediated through his or her body and the experience of being joined with it. Spiritually, the human body is the sacrament of a person. A true erotic desire recognizes the sacrament for what it is—something that points beyond itself to a profound unity between persons.

Augustine is the theologian most credited with establishing the central Christian attitudes to sex. Sadly, Augustine identified sinful concupiscence with sexual desire, which he interpreted as tainted at its very roots. Despite that, he did understand rightly that eros love is at the heart of the search for God. "Our hearts are restless, Lord, until they find their repose in you" (*Confessions*, 12). Augustine knew that desire was not something we could or should uproot but rather was an essential mark of our humanity and our belonging to God. Instead, he suggested that the objects of desire or of eros need to be ordered in accordance with their true relationship to God. The erotic is well ordered if it is radically open to the transcendent. Whatever criticisms may be laid at Augustine's door, this aspect of his thought has great merit.

In our experiences of sexual desire love is not primarily universal, even if it is ultimately open to universality. Sexual desire is particular, passionate and embodied. In the same way, God, incarnate in the man Jesus, is revealed as passionately engaged with the particular circumstances of our world and with all people in particular. Sexual desire, if it runs deep, is similarly self-giving and committed. Yet the idea that the body language of human love is a concrete articulation of the love of God revealed in Jesus Christ seems pretty daring to some people. How can we compare the love of God with the urgent, painful and sometimes wounding experiences of human longing and passion? And so, it has been commonplace to separate sex from the incarnation. Is it not the case that many people think that Jesus was like us in all things but ... sex? But through the incarnation God refuses to be seen as a proposition or abstraction. Instead,

God becomes human in a physical and therefore sexual person, who experienced pleasure, pain and need.

The scandal is not in linking sex to Jesus or to God's self-giving, but in the fact that our Christian faith, while based on a particular instance of embodied love, has so little place for the religious significance of the erotic. Theological discussion has usually been limited to sexual ethics—how an essentially physical reality can find outlets in safely prescribed contexts. If you think this statement is exaggerated, I invite you to ask yourself how many people you know, including yourself, who would tell their spiritual history in terms based partly on sexual experience. How many of us, too, would see our sexual growth (pain or passion) as intimately associated with our following of Christ or as liberating us to enter more deeply into the desire of God?

We all need to move beyond our tendency to underestimate the erotic and reduce it to the fulfillment of social needs. Sexuality is about more than cementing stable families and reproducing the human race. It is this kind of reductionism, at least as much as a fear of bodily powers, that led sexual renunciation rather than sexual experience to become *the* way of spiritual growth and, therefore, the privileged icon of God's self-gift in Jesus. Spiritual elites "reproduced" through attracting vocations rather than through sexual interaction! As a result, sexual union became the province of the "secular," if not the profane, rather than of truly spiritual people. It is only in more recent times that a committed sexual relationship has been capable of being understood as vocational.

If we go back to the story of the origins of Christian asceticism, to the desert fathers and mothers of Syria, Palestine and Egypt, we see that sexual temptation in itself was often treated in a rather matter of fact way. Sexual desire was seen, at least implicitly, especially in terms of a sharp antithesis between the "world" and the "desert." To flee the world was not so much to flee *sex* or the body. But it did involve leaving a precise set of social relationships and constraints—for example, the drive toward marriage, child-rearing and conscription into the settled land and its culture. The ideal of living "like the angels," who do not marry (assumed to be the lot of resurrected human beings as well), did not really originate in a concern for physical purity however it may have been interpreted later. The assumed life of the angels had more to do with a conception of perfected human society which, it was thought, would be voluntary and harmonious rather than based on purely conventional structures.

The above reference to the ultimate state of resurrected people reminds us that where an overbalanced emphasis on the afterlife has appeared in religious thinking, the inevitable result is a devaluation of the erotic. It is perhaps not surprising that the Hebrew scriptures, which have a less well-developed belief in bodily survival after death, are happier to emphasize the positive qualities in the present life of the erotic in relation to the sacred. This raises important questions for us as contemporary Christians. Can we experience, even if only partially, what is of absolute value in the here and now? Are we capable of reading spiritual depth into the enjoyment of all good things as God's blessings and God's playfulness? Or is *real* fulfillment and joy only to be found in the hereafter—a better life in a better place? If the latter is the case, we will tend to sacrifice what is seen as dubious pleasure now for perfect joy later.

Intimacy

Here we are, you and I, and I hope a third, Christ is in our midst....

God is friendship.... But still what is true of charity, I surely do not hesitate to grant to friendship, since "he that abides in friendship, abides in God, and God in him" (Aelred of Rievaulx, *Spiritual Friendship*, 1:1, 69 and 70).

These words of Aelred, a twelfth-century Yorkshire Cistercian, remind us that, once again, it is important not to reduce our understanding of sexuality to genital activity, as if this one area provides the total meaning of love and intimacy. Sexuality in its broadest sense covers our whole experience of embodiment. Affective sexuality involves a huge area of feelings and emotions that move us toward other people. And this is true of all kinds of relationships, including those of single people. It is, if you like, what enables all of us to express tenderness, closeness, compassion and openness to touch. It follows that intimacy is not something reserved to certain categories of people (that is, the married). Single people, including those committed for various reasons to celibacy, are equally called to intimacy with other human beings. Those who are already within committed relationships also need to discover how to become appropriately intimate, in a non-genital way, with people who are not their partners. Equally, without some capacity for non-genital intimacy, heterosexuals would find it hard to develop close relationships with members of the same sex and homosexuals with members of the opposite sex.

The call to intimacy that we all experience at different points in our lives is an invitation to take risks. For all human love can come to an end, may deceive, is partial, is not totally and finally reliable. Yet, our capacity and need for intimacy is a call to find *within* this risk of human loving the love of God that is total, constant and faithful. Deep human friendship is a powerful contribution, arguably the most powerful, to a loving union with God. The call to intimacy also involves a realization that however much two people love each other they will never possess or own each other, nor will they ever fully know each other. There is always an area of inalienable strangeness in the other person. There is forever the possibility of greater depth, of "more," in all relationships.

Whether we are single or in a committed, exclusive relationship, the Christian insights about eros love and agape love remind us that to become complete we are all called to seek the eventual integration of particular and universal love. Only within our experiences of intimacy with other people, whether genital or not, may we learn a way of being fully present both to ourselves and to others rather than being superficial and remote in our emotional lives. The risk of intimacy, rather than the apparent security of emotional detachment, reveals the truth of ourselves, teaches us about availability and educates us in truthful self-disclosure. Of all human experiences it is the one most likely to provoke real change in us.

Another thing that the search for love reveals is the need for a balance between solitude and intimacy. What we find in our human relationships we will also find in our relationship with God. To say that solitude and intimacy need to remain in balance is to affirm two things. First, we need a sufficient degree of rootedness in ourselves before we can move outward to others in a non-abusive way. An Indian friend commented of Western "seekers" wandering around the subcontinent at the beginning of the 1980s that only those who know where they come from, where they belong, are safe to travel. This comment could just as well be applied to the journey of love as to geographical travel. *Solitude* describes that necessary place and time of waiting where we learn how to receive—ourselves, God and other people—in disinterested love. The ability to receive in such a self-transcending way does not come easily. To learn to wait and then to learn the fruitful communication of intimacy is always painful, for it involves a stripping away of unreal expectations and selfish demands and yet, at the same time, a deepening and sharpening of true desire.

Second, an intimacy that is spiritually healthy always allows the other person to remain securely in his or her own space. The German poet Rainer Rilke suggested that real love does not consist in "merging" but means "that two solitudes protect and border and salute each other" (Rilke 1954, 59). That seems a wonderful description not only of human intimacy but of God's intimacy with us revealed in and through human loving.

Liberation from Private Will

If we turn our thoughts again to the desert ascetics of the early centuries, we can see that they understood well the greatest human emotional battle: how to overcome our divided hearts. In concrete terms this is the struggle in daily experience to be liberated from a false and destructive individuality—the tyranny of private will. Paradoxically, abstinence from sexual relations was seen by early Christians as really only important as a servant of this greater struggle. The conflicts we all experience with the "desires of the flesh" simply reveal the more deeply rooted, essential flaws of the heart. The early ascetics sensed an absolute quality in the choice of sexual abstinence that made it a powerful symbol of the boundary between the spiritual innocence they desired and complicity with things of this world. The early ascetics were considered to be heroes not so much because they had risen totally above the needs of the flesh (which was never the case anyway) but because their bodily discipline gained them hearts that were all of a piece.

Today these same desert values, which can be summed up as the desire for singleness of heart, are increasingly being rediscovered as the ideal at the center of intimacy and sexual union. Many Christians are also convinced that the wider world needs to hear a new word about sexuality and its potential spiritual depths in order to counteract the superficiality of much media presentation. However, there is a growing realization that traditional Christian spirituality, unlike Judaism or Islam at their best, has generally failed to provide any explicit underpinning for the spiritual quality of sexuality. It seems that we need a new dimension to our tradition in order to create the possibility of a deeper life in God within rather than outside full human sexual life.

When we allow ourselves to become aware of our sexual desire, we gain important indicators of the deeper and more complex levels of our existence. This awareness offers the possibility of growing into maturity not only psychologically but also spiritually. For example, our experience of sexual arousal tends to be seen as primarily an instinctual and physical force. However, it is also a matter of personal power, and as such is an opportunity for choice and discernment. This becomes an important context for opting into a way of existence based on values. In other words, we may be frequently aroused, but we choose whether to act upon those feelings or not. Cultivating awareness of what comes into play as we are aroused, and as we choose to act or not act, is a deepening experience. Gradually we learn to respond to arousal not with compulsive behavior but by choosing options based on self-awareness and the awareness of other people. This, in the best sense, is the moral dimension of sex. It is essentially linked to our inner life in the Spirit rather than to abstract norms and external guidance. As we learn what we desire (both what we enjoy *and* what we need in the broadest sense) and learn to communicate that desire, we come to live increasingly in relation to it rather than to compulsion on the one hand or moral guilt on the other. This is the process of becoming a sexually mature person.

Sexuality is, as it were, the testing ground of the integration or fragmentation of our personalities. We do not want to ignore the reality of sexual pathologies by retreating into an idealized view of human love and sex. The very power of sex makes it impossible for it to be a neutral reality. Wrongly directed sex (as well as the sexual expression of our wrong directions) tends to be compulsive and destructive. Without doubt sex can bind us and make us incapable of fulfilling our responsibilities to ourselves and others. It can also be insatiable, preventing us from ever feeling fulfilled. This is likely to make us either bitter with our partner who has "failed" us or angry about our apparent inability to find satisfactory partners at all. But the essential point here is that conflicted sexuality and misplaced sexual behavior are indicators of much broader problems of maturity, freedom and spiritual health.

The converse is true of a joyful and balanced sexual awareness, self-acceptance and self-communication—and indeed self-transcendence, in which we find our greatest pleasure in the pleasure of the other. Equality, mutuality and reciprocity are the hallmarks of a mature, free, non-possessive, non-abusive love. The depths of intimacy, including sexual union, are profoundly kenotic or self-giving in their direction. We are moved toward a shedding of our false selves and come to live and act more and more from within the truth of who we are. We grow in our capacity to be available, to be appropriately disclosed, to be strong yet vulnerable, deeply moved to change rather than to stand stubbornly and fearfully in the safe and known.

To give and to receive sexually has a sacramental quality as long as it is truly aspires to be a gift of *self* and a joyful receiving of another person rather than merely an exchange of bodily stimulations. Spirit touches spirit. We might borrow the old catechism language about sacraments, "it is an outward sign of inward grace," of a deeper inner reality. Appropriate sexual body language is a sacrament of Real Presence—both the true and unashamed presence of one person to another and, within that and cementing that self-disclosure, the Real Presence of the indwelling God. "This is my body—my life—given for you." "And they recognized him in the breaking of the bread." And we may recognize God, too, in the breaking open of bodies, the breaking open of self, for each other.

Sexual union is eucharistic, a liturgy that may heal and restore loving partners to a spiritual centeredness. When we freely unite ourselves to another, we come to know ourselves at the same time as profoundly self-possessed, rather than invaded or stolen. Here, desire becomes more than a physical urge and is discovered to be that power within us that enables us to overcome our fears of absorption. The acceptance of our body by another, and our acceptance of theirs, in intimate touch and mutual delight, is ultimately transformed into a deepening sense of the wholesomeness of our *person*. As we truly come into possession of our self, and learn to dwell in the self, we are also led into a movement beyond self to the other. And as we come truly to dwell in the particular and personal love of the other person, we are led even further by that same movement of openness. This does not occur without pain and struggle. But through deep intimacy we move slowly toward the horizon of non-exclusive, universal love where, as in God, eros and agape are found ultimately to be one.

Sexual Union and Union with God

There is a beautiful account of spiritual communion in sexual intimacy in the extraordinary diary for the years 1941-43 of the Dutch Jew Etty Hillesum:

> Perhaps that is the only real way of kissing a man. Not just out of sensuality but also from a desire to breathe for one moment through a single mouth. So that a single breath passes through both....

> And then for a short hour we had shared one breath as I had been wanting to do for many, many weeks. And I had rested so confidently and with so much surrender in his arms and yet full of sensual tension. But above everything else there was that shared breath. And in that short hour so much strength flowed into me that I believed I could live on it my whole life long (Hillesum 1985, 117).

A number of people whom I know have found those words to be a powerful expression of their own experiences, at least at moments, of their sexual relations.

In the context of my own gradual awakening to the spiritual power of sexuality, one of the spiritual books that had the greatest effect was the profound and beautifully written *Yes to God* by the late Alan Ecclestone. Among other things, it daringly (or so I thought in the mid-1970s) had a chapter on "Spirituality and Sexual Love." Perhaps that simple fact was for me, in the long term, more important than the content of Ecclestone's words, but a number of his phrases and images remain with me. First, sexuality represents our passion to become engaged. Second, it is "a great hunger," "a perception of beauty," "an intense pleasure." Yes, all of those things, but ordered in such a way that "it challenges those divided by it to seek and find at another level a unity of being." Most powerfully of all, Ecclestone concluded,

> The primitive impulse to deify sexual love was not wholly misguided; it has all the features of great mystical experience, abandon, ecstasy, polarity, dying, rebirth and perfect union.... It prompts between human beings those features characteristic of prayer; a noticing, a paying attention, a form of address, a yearning to communicate at ever deeper levels of being, an attempt to reach a certain communion with the other (Ecclestone 1975, 88).

If much mystical literature traditionally had used the language of sexual union to describe our relationship with God, Ecclestone turned this, as it were, on its head. He used the language and experience of mysticism and prayer to express with great power the fullest potential of sexual union.

When sexual union is the consummation of deep, exclusive and faithful love between two people, it may be a sacrament of that union with God, and in God with all that is, for which God has created and redeemed us. Shared sexual joy, as a step toward God rather than as a substitute for it, is a genuine act of worship, a genuine prayer. Etty

Hillesum learned a great deal about this from her close friend
and lover Julius Spier:

> To him everything is of a piece, he does not separate
> the physical from the spiritual and feels so close and
> familiar to me precisely because his life is so much
> more coherent than mine (Hillesum 1985, 111).

Of course, there are other kinds of human communion
and communication that have something of the same possibility, but the sexual union between faithful lovers involves
an intensity, an abandonment, yes, even an ecstasy, that
makes this potentially the most powerful of symbols.

In his unusual attempt to reintegrate sexuality with
religious mysticism (*The Meaning of Love*), the controversial
Russian theologian Vladimir Solovyov pointed out that the
"higher" animals paid less attention to pure multiplication
of the species than the "lower" ones. Solovyov suggested that
what he called "sex love" figured more strongly wherever
the feeling of love for a unique person took on an unconditional importance—unconditional, not least, as to the
person's capacity to be a good procreator! The desirability of
the other is not dependent on her or his "usefulness"
(Solovyov 1945).

The ecstatic, even mystical reading of sexual union has
historically found more acceptance in parts of the Jewish
tradition than in Christianity. In some quarters the Song of
Songs, while still associated with Passover time because it
was taken to reflect the mutual love between God and the
people of Israel, was also granted an explicitly interpersonal
interpretation. Thus it was sometimes read on the Sabbath
evening as a reminder that the beginning of the Sabbath saw
the arrival of a "Bride" who was to be welcomed. Sexual
intercourse between spouses was also encouraged on the
Sabbath night. To make love out of the fullness, relaxation
and joy of Sabbath was the earthly counterpart of the holy
union that occurred on the Sabbath evening between the

shechinah (the indwelling presence of God, sometimes seen as the feminine aspect) and the masculine aspect of God.

To draw a parallel between the sexual act and mystical union with God, as some Jewish traditions, Solovyov and Ecclestone do, should not appear blasphemous to Christians. If there is a blasphemy it lies, rather, in the fact that the sexual act has been so downgraded that we find the parallel disconcerting. The intensity of union with a partner is no longer naturally associated with our calling in Christ to be drawn into the life of God, or what the Eastern Christian tradition calls "deification." Nor does union suggest the possibility of a participation by loving partners in the ecstatic, creative outpouring of God. This is far more than simply being procreators in a purely biological sense. To have such a "high" view of participation in creation naturally has its painful side. Apparent "failures," such as miscarriages, are always psychologically painful. However, there is in addition a *spiritual* pain involved when a couple's sexual relations include an intense sense of participating in God's creative action.

It seems to me that the contemporary criticism of traditional patriarchy in the West opens up the possibility of arriving at a more positive evaluation of sex and of its conscious re-integration into the sacred. A patriarchal way of seeing things tends to give sacred significance mainly to the biological aspects of sex. Thus, particular emphasis has been placed, at least implicitly, on the active male fertilization of passive matter provided by a female incubator. The mystical-sacred dimension of sexual union is effectively diminished in such an unequal understanding of sexuality. Instead of stepping back in awe at the mystery of sex, we have also tended to prescribe how it should be conducted and thus to reduce it. This diminishment of sex is true both of pornography (sex is only for pleasure) and of a great deal of Christian moral teaching (sex is only to make babies). When compared to a richer vision, both views are revealed as reductionist and functional, sometimes to a neurotic degree.

A Crossing of Boundaries

Various writers have suggested that sex and death are interrelated, biologically, psychologically and spiritually. This makes a great deal of sense. For the religious person both death and sex are channels of union with God and/or another person that involve the dissolution of the boundaries that normally identify us as individuals, distinct from other people and all that surrounds us. The dissolution of boundaries can take place without loss of personal identity. In this way both death and sex share in the traditional characteristics of mysticism. Without doubt, to step beyond the familiar boundaries is always a risky business. Perhaps this is why death, sex and mysticism have been viewed with equal fear and suspicion at times within the Christian community!

For adults, sexual relations may at times be a major source of ecstatic experiences. However, we have been conditioned not to think of them in this way. To do so would be to encroach on the domain of the sacred that traditionally was presumed to lie beyond such profane things as sex. There has also been a tendency in Christian mystical theory to limit the "ecstatic" to a very narrow band of extraordinary experiences that are given to very few people. Fortunately, there is a contrary movement today, accepted, albeit with caution, even by more conservative religious writers, to understand mysticism as a much more widespread and everyday reality than has traditionally been appreciated. If this is so, then sexual union has the potential to be one of the primary God-given channels in human life for such experience.

Whether interpreted broadly or more narrowly, ecstasy may best be understood precisely as an experience of the temporary dissolution of the normal boundaries of perception and living. Etty Hillesum at times experienced intimacy in a similar way.

He leant against the wall of Dicky's room and I leant
gently and lightly against him, just as I had done on
countless similar occasions in the past, but this time
it suddenly felt as if the sky had fallen as in a Greek
tragedy. For a moment my senses were totally confused and I felt as though I was standing with him in
the center of infinite space—pervaded by threats but
also filled with eternity. In that moment a great
change took place within us, for ever (Hillesum 1985,
172-73).

Ecstasy is a moment in which some otherwise distant
reality is glimpsed as here and now and at one with oneself.
This is a peak experience. Whether in the context of contemplation or sexual relations, it is something that it is
dangerous and damaging to grasp for its own sake. It is, after
all, possible to become addicted to altered states of consciousness, whether produced by drugs or by sex. But such
addiction is to mistake the means for the end. Peak experiences have their place in any fully human life and are *not* to be
viewed with suspicion. But in contemplative mysticism the
particular experiences exist in order to transform the whole
of life. So, the ecstasy of sexual union, and the temporary
dissolution of boundaries involved with it, serve the more
general transformation of two people and their growing
together into union on every level of their being. In other
words, the unitive "glimpses" that sexual or contemplative
ecstasy provides serve to deepen our personalities and to
deepen our perceptions of the way reality is.

Sexual ecstasy, while involving some form of bodily
self-giving, is more than bodily in the sense that it concerns
the blending together of two people. In other words, it is
profoundly associated with intimacy. Intimacy with another
human being (of which bodily self-giving is a powerful but
not exclusive symbol) is the privileged context for experienc-
ing God as immanence.

We need to maintain a certain delicacy here. As with God's relationship with us, human intimacy involves holding in proper balance an appropriate dissolution of personal boundaries and yet the continued respect for personal space. It is an unfortunate fact, of which we are being made increasingly aware these days, that the sexual crossing of boundaries has often been violent and abusive. At the heart of most cases of sexual abuse, including rape, lies the desire to gain power over another human being. Sexual violation of boundaries seems to be used to meet a number of needs that have little to do with real sexual desire, let alone with love.

True human desire, just like God's desire for us, is respectfully attuned both to the self and to the partner. Each person may be lost in the other, but individual boundaries are not abused or invaded. Each person freely allows them to be crossed in a way that enhances both partners rather than destroys either's identity.

FIVE

Desire and Choosing

To reach satisfaction in all
desire its possession in nothing.
To come to possess all
desire the possession of nothing.
To arrive at being all
desire to be nothing.
To come to the knowledge of all
desire the knowledge of nothing.
To come to the pleasure you have not
you must go by a way in which you enjoy not.
To come to the knowledge you have not
you must go by a way in which you know not.
To come to the possession you have not
you must go by a way in which you possess not.
To come to be what you are not
you must go by a way in which you are not
(John of the Cross, *The Ascent of Mount Carmel*,
Book 1, chapter 13, 11).

Whether we are familiar with the original language of John
of the Cross or are more used to the paraphrase by T. S. Eliot
in his poem "East Coker," the way to spiritual perfection
presented in the quotation above could be interpreted as one
of unremitting and unattractive negativity. However, the

journey suggested by John of the Cross is one of desire. And
desire, with its connotation of incompleteness, is instead an
image of movement and change. From childhood onward we
all have to learn that to grow up involves leaving the familiar
and controllable and travelling through places and experiences that are not familiar.

Yet, paradoxically, it is also in this journey through the
loss of childhood certainties and securities that we come
more and more to a firm sense of our own identity and to the
ability to make autonomous choices. In the process of matur-
ing we hopefully move, whether consciously or not, from
fulfilling the expectations and desires of others to a greater
realization of our own desires and the appropriateness of
choosing for ourselves. If we are unwilling to leave the
security of what is known, we will never arrive anywhere.
"To reach satisfaction in all, desire its possession in nothing."
If we cannot let go of trying to accumulate many different
things, we will never discover what having "all" means.

To Live Is to Choose

To be truly alive is continually to make choices. There is
a sense in which we come to be as persons through our many
experiences of choosing. It is a paradox that we can only
move toward what John of the Cross calls "satisfaction in all"
by making choices, for to choose also, and always, means to
abandon something, to exclude other courses of action. "To
reach satisfaction in all, desire its possession in ... *no thing*."

Ignatius Loyola has a very different kind of spirituality
from John of the Cross. Yet in his teaching on discernment he
understood something of the same dynamic. He wrote in his
Spiritual Exercises of the need always to desire "the more,"
and for "indifference" or "detachment." It is possible to
understand the words in rather negative terms. However,
understood properly, "indifference" and "detachment" are
extremely positive, because they are concerned with reaching an ever greater degree of inner freedom. Such freedom

cannot be artificially constructed. It is a gift of God's grace. Yet it is what is needed in order to grow inwardly from the level of immediate desires to that of our deepest desire. There is a journey into the cave of the heart where our essential self and God both dwell. The problem is that we are often the prisoners of our immediate and urgent neediness. Our tendency to accumulate possessions, for example, can be a desperate sign of our fear of being nothing, or becoming nothing. It is all too easy to mistake the temporary assuaging of our needs for "satisfaction in all."

So choosing (or discerning how to choose) does not simply involve detached, rational thinking, even though there has to be a place for that. We have, in a sense, to dive headlong into our experience, into our desires, in order to discern truly. For to discern our deepest desire involves an act of commitment as well as an experience of enlightenment. To discern is not, on the one hand, purely a deeper level of awareness or, on the other, merely a decision. It ultimately involves moving further toward a harmonious relationship with who we most genuinely are as people. This in turn means coming to a realistic acceptance of how we are situated in the world of places and events. Discernment, in other words, is a matter of continually reaching out for integrity.

The diary of Etty Hillesum, leading up to her departure for Auschwitz in 1943, records her painful yet joyful struggle to reach the greatest possible degree of spiritual integrity. Etty's whole diary might be seen as the record of a process of discernment and choice—increasingly from within her deepest self as well as from within the truth of her circumstances and relationships. In this unfolding self-awareness and self-acceptance, Etty also encountered God with an intensity that was perhaps mystical.

> I sometimes actually drop to my knees beside my bed, even on a cold winter night. And I listen in to myself, allow myself to be led, not by anything on the outside, but by what wells up from within (Hillesum 1985, 81).

To discover the truth of our heart's desire is also to recognize something familiar, even if it is to know it explicitly for the first time. It is in some sense, therefore, a return to the sources of our being. Our desires have the capacity to reveal truth, for the latter is not ultimately some abstract reality to be reached by means of conceptual thinking alone. As the famous Thai Buddhist master Achaan Chaa suggests, "At some point your heart will tell itself what to do."

Realizing Our Destiny

Without suggesting a fatalistic view of human life, this approach to choosing has a great deal to do with coming to understand and then grasping wholeheartedly our particular "destiny." Once we have understood our destiny for what it is, there is a kind of inevitability about it. This is because it is so intimately associated with our identities as individual persons. It is not something imposed from outside by a God who acts like some puppet-master of the universe, making demands of us irrespective of our circumstances. On the contrary, destiny is "what lies in us"; it is our special gift. This does not make it painless for, like Etty Hillesum in Nazi-occupied Holland, it may impel us to make courageous choices that even our closest friends cannot fully understand.

> And it is right to feel sick and confused and unsettled for once, like today, full of cold fear and uncertainty, and a sigh of "Good God, child, what are you letting yourself in for?" But also a growing sense of self-certainty. I have matured enough to assume my "destiny," to cease living an accidental life.... Now I have a right to a "destiny." It is no longer a romantic dream or the thirst for adventure, or for love, all of which can drive you to commit mad and irresponsible acts. No, it is a terrible, sacred, inner seriousness, difficult and at the same time inevitable (Hillesum 1985, 138).

The spiritual journey mapped out in their distinctive ways by John of the Cross and Ignatius Loyola demands courage; we must act from the heart by being attuned to the truth of our desires. To reach that kind of attunement is not a simple matter. There is ultimately no method by which we can learn how to discern effectively and infallibly on every occasion. The key to discernment is not technique but the focused intensity of our desire. It is a matter of attitude and of relationships—the quality of how we relate to our own self, to other people, to created reality, to God. Etty Hillesum talked of a mysterious inner regulator growing within her:

> I still believe I have an inner regulator, which warns me every time I take the wrong path by bringing on a "depression." If only I remain honest and open with myself and determined enough to become what I must be and to do what my conscience commands, then everything will turn out all right (Hillesum 1985, 203).

Having said this, it is possible to place ourselves more in a position where this quality of relatedness may be deepened. Meditation in all its forms ultimately seeks to cultivate attentiveness and awareness. Both of these are vital ingredients of a discerning heart. Yet, sometimes it takes considerable patience and trust to believe in this kind of meditative "doing nothing." The contemporary American writer Ken Wilber in a book about his wife Treya and her spiritual journey quotes her as saying:

> When I wonder why I sit ... I say to myself that I sit to express myself as I am at this moment.... Perhaps later purpose will come clear ... perhaps purpose is already here, unfolding as I go (Wilber 1991, 162).

Sometimes the birth of converted attitudes and of deepened ways of relating has to take place in darkness, in patient waiting. Light somehow needs the darkness in order to be known. Without embracing the darkness we miss the

light. Darkness and waiting sharpen desire, test its depths
and lead us to a point where we simply have to let go. We
find so often that meaning lies in the very waiting. Sadly, for
most of us, waiting is extremely difficult, especially in a
culture where immediate satisfaction, and simple methods
to achieve it, are presented as of overwhelming importance.

From Many Desires to Deepest Desire

Because discernment is a journey, we will find ourselves
moving, slowly perhaps, from an initial awareness of a multitude of desires, wants and needs (and probably a relatively
undiscriminating search for their satisfaction) to the deeper
levels of our self. We may also see this as a movement from
awareness of desire to responsible action in the light of that
awareness. However, it is important to remember that the
other levels of desire we encounter and pass through on the
way are not irrelevant. We will never come to know our
deepest desire except through attention to the many desires.
We need to acknowledge our multitude of feelings, experiences and needs, which exist not so much in a harmonious,
inclusive way as in a confusing one. "I have so many desires,
I don't know what to do with them." But it is in fearless
engagement with this confusion, rather than simply by some
activity of our rational, detached intellect, that we move
toward our center. The many desires are necessary staging
posts on a journey toward what is most true in us. Ignatius
Loyola expressed something of this idea when he suggested
that we should relate to created things "to the extent that they
help us toward our end" (*Spiritual Exercises*, No. 23).

The scriptural story of the Samaritan woman at the well
in the Gospel of John, chapter 4, provides us with a striking
image of the relationship between our initial needs and our
deep desires. The woman is led by the conversation with
Jesus from an immediate sense of needing fresh water to her
deeper desire for "the spring of water within, welling up for
eternal life." Even through the pain of being confronted with

her many failures in human relationships, the Samaritan woman approaches a more truthful sense of her identity and of the power of God that is being made available to her. The woman also learned by confronting her history of relationships that to attend to desires and to discern among them are parts of the process of becoming more passionately focused on what is life-giving rather than destructive. This, once again, is what the author of *The Cloud of Unknowing* implies by our need to stand in "naked intent," and what Ignatius Loyola means by suggesting in his *Spiritual Exercises* that we should ask for what we desire at the beginning of prayer.

Different Kinds of Desire?

When we think about the discernment of our desires, it is important to remember that each of us is a single, unified human being, even though we have many dimensions. The problem is that in practice we tend to distinguish between the emotional, intellectual, physical and spiritual parts of ourselves. And so we divide up our "passions" according to their association with one particular aspect of our human existence. Yet, these dimensions of our personality, and the kinds of desires associated with them, exist in a continuous interdependence. Thus, the way we treat our bodies affects the deepest longings of our spirits. And our spiritual desires find their expression in our immediate feelings and in our bodily reactions. Over the last few years I have learned, thanks to my spiritual director and various therapist friends, to pay much more attention to the way that changes in my body are indicators of spiritual well-being or spiritual confusion. It is important to grasp that our so-called spiritual desires do not exist in a separate compartment of life. The whole of our life is spiritual. We cannot say that any desire is irrelevant to the process of spiritual growth and discernment. Every kind of desire is touched by the Spirit of God in some sense, even if it is capable of being misdirected.

One of the most common, and also most difficult, human experiences is that of being pulled in opposite directions by apparently contradictory desires. This is particularly true when these desires, in the first instance, seem good and important. We find ourselves powerfully, almost willy-nilly, drawn toward people, objects and ideals that are not merely diverse but sometimes incompatible. We are sometimes moved by passions that fragment us, perhaps violently so. In this context discernment is the way of sifting through a confusion of desires in order that our lives may be shaped by the best of them. But the "best of them" does not imply that we live in a two-tier universe in which certain types of human desires are inherently better, or that "the best" are immediately recognizable. We are all the products, and sometimes the victims, of our upbringing and environment. Sometimes we have to struggle against assuming that we must always make certain kinds of choices if we are to be "good Christians."

Great Desires

Certain desires have the potential to shape our most serious choices and therefore to give direction to our lives. These are what Ignatius Loyola termed "great desires." Active commitment to a great cause falls into that category; for example, to be with Christ and to play a part, with others, in establishing the Kingdom of God throughout the world. The self-giving of disinterested love—or the desire for it—is another. At the other end of the spectrum, some desires merely speak of instant needs or immediate satisfaction in matters that are petty rather than life-directional.

It is, of course, only too easy to mistake the desire for personal satisfaction for the answer to life's mystery, but that is what the art of discernment is all about. As a process, discernment enables us, in the first instance, to be aware of and to accept the full range of desires that we experience. From this starting point we are slowly led to understand the way in which our desires vary greatly in their quality. Certain desires, or ways of desiring, if we follow them through, will tend to push toward a dispersion of our spiritual and psychic energy or a fragmentation of our attention, experience and personality. Other desires seem to promise a greater concentration of energy and a harmonious centeredness. It is sometimes initially confusing that the less helpful or healthy desires appear to be more strikingly attractive because they make us feel good. In other words, the direction and potential of our desires is not always immediately evident. To come to appreciate these things demands patient reflection.

Desire and Ignatian Discernment

Reflection on our feeling experiences, with a view to choosing the greater good, is the central feature of the Christian tradition of discernment. One of the most effective summaries of this tradition is in the *Spiritual Exercises* of Ignatius Loyola. Perhaps the most helpful element of his teaching is the importance he gives to our ability to identify two basic kinds of affective experience, which he calls consolation and desolation, and to act appropriately in relation to each (Nos. 313-36). This is not just a matter of our undertaking intense introspection in order to uncover all our possible motivations, even if the beginning of discernment consists of recognizing various movements or desires within our heart and psyche.

When we reflect upon desires as the bases for our choices, we may spend rather a lot of time trying to work out where such desires come from or what inspires them. This is not always easy. In fact, for Ignatius, it is much less helpful to search for the roots of our actions than to focus on the direction in which our desires and longings are moving and the deeper moods that they create. Discernment is all about recognizing the energies that drive us. What kind of energy is being released? As someone said to me recently, Ignatius recognized that we can experience two kinds of "buzz" and that their immediate intensity is not the most reliable in-

dicator of their ultimate truthfulness. So, when Ignatius
Loyola wrote about "inner movements," he was not simply
referring to the depth of disturbance or the strength of feelings. He was suggesting that all desires and feelings have a
direction. Some desires are life-giving and others ultimately
destructive.

The basic characteristics of consolation are an increase
of love of God as well as a deepening of human love, an
increase of hope and faith, an interior joy, an attraction
toward the spiritual, a deep tranquillity and peace. It is
vitally important to remember that Ignatius is not talking
about the *immediately* pleasurable. There exists something
that might be called "hard" consolation. This involves a
healthy realization of our own brokenness as well as a shar-
pened sensitivity to the pain of the world. There is often a
paradox in consolation. "Interior joy" or "deep peace,"
produced by a realization of the power, love and faithfulness
of God, may in fact go hand in hand with a great deal of
external disturbance and pain.

Perhaps one of the sharpest experiences I had of what
this kind of consolation might mean came while I was strug-
gling to be alongside a close friend during the final stages of
cancer. She went through several weeks of terrible anguish,
spiritual pain and intense fear. All of us around her, family
and friends, found this very hard to bear. But gradually,
although the physical discomfort and decline grew worse,
my friend was moved into a deep reassurance and a recon-
ciliation with so many of the fractured experiences of her life.
Ultimately she reached a contentment with dying, characterized by a readiness to let go and a deep desire for God.

In contrast to consolation, desolation may initially feel
quite pleasant and attractive. However, whether on the surface or deep down, desolation ultimately reveals itself as
drawing us in destructive directions. Ignatius suggests that
its key characteristics are opposite to those of consolation. So,
there is a decrease of faith or hope or the capacity to love truly.
There is turmoil and confusion at a deep level rather than

merely surface disturbance. There is a tendency toward impulsive behavior, especially in the direction of emotional or physical self-indulgence. Other feelings that Ignatius lists include listlessness, tepidity, unhappiness and a sense of separation from God. It is too simple, however, to say that desolation is the same as the experience of depression or "feeling bad." Psychological depression and spiritual desolation may overlap at times, but they are not precisely the same thing. There are people who suffer from lifelong clinical depression but who may, nonetheless, be said to be in consolation because they never quite lose touch with the love and faithfulness of God as their deepest truth.

Throughout his *Spiritual Exercises* Ignatius Loyola returns again and again to the subject of desire, which is always ordered toward a deeper and more healthy way of choosing. For Ignatius, the spiritual journey is essentially away from fragmentation and toward harmony, from the surface to the center, from spiritual imprisonment toward inner freedom. The whole point of our "spiritual activities" is to be gradually rid of what he calls "disordered affections" (No. 1). This movement away from disordered feelings and needs that tend to entrap me is what Ignatius means by the somewhat unattractive word "indifference" (No. 23). This is not a cold absence of feeling or a dispassionate detachment. "Indifference" involves reaching out toward our deepest desire, which is to be what we were created for. Once we have recognized the disorder in our inclinations, it is possible to help the process of freedom along by consciously seeking to focus our attention, as well as our actions, on the opposite (No. 16).

However, it is clear that Ignatius Loyola does not see the answer to discernment and spiritual growth essentially in terms of human effort and will power. On the contrary, while we may dispose ourselves, open ourselves and center ourselves, it is God alone who puts proper order into our desires. Ignatius also recognized wisely that we cannot honestly desire to take a life-enhancing direction overnight. So he suggested that we may be capable only of desiring to have the desire! And that spark, that chink in our defensive armor, is all that God needs. Positively, if we engage with our desires on this journey toward spiritual freedom, it means moving from a mainly intellectual perception of God toward an inner "savoring" of God's reality in the depths of our being (No. 2). It also demands that we enter into the journey with deep generosity and commitment (No. 5). However, Ignatius warns us that this should not be confused with an intensity of fervor that might lead us to unconsidered or hasty responses (No. 14). Sometimes, as Mary did in the story of the annunciation in the Gospel of Luke, we need to check the credentials of our apparent inner experiences of God. Perhaps we need even to interrogate God before we act on what seem to be God's promptings or give our wholehearted commitment to them!

> But her whole body pulls away.
> Only her head, already haloed, bows,
> acquiescing. And though she will, she's not yet said,
> *Behold, I am the handmaid of the Lord,*
> as Botticelli, in his great pity,
> lets her refuse, accept, refuse, and think again
> (Hudgins 1991, "The Cestello Annunciation").

Meditations of Desire

Two crucial meditations in the second phase, or what Ignatius Loyola calls the "Second Week," of the *Spiritual Exercises* seem to me to illustrate graphically different levels or qualities of desire. The Meditation on Three Classes of Persons (Nos. 149-57) and the Meditation on Three Ways of Being Humble (Nos. 165-68) are associated, in the dynamic of the Exercises, with what Ignatius describes as making "an election." An election means choosing a way of life that is single-heartedly concerned with "the purpose for which I am created" (who I am) and with "desiring to serve God" (my sense of ultimate meaning).

In the Meditation on Three Classes of Persons, the different levels of desire are illustrated by three people who have each received a large sum of money. The first person recognizes at a certain level the need to be free of unhealthy dependence on the money, yet does nothing at all about it. The second person desires the same freedom but equally desires to retain the money—an attempt to balance two conflicting desires. The third person desires to be free but, interestingly, does not mind whether the money is kept or not. The desire for freedom is deep enough that it can cope with either having money or not having money.

In the other meditation, the first way of being humble describes the minimum level, or quality, of desire. This relates to a belief that we will be saved, and that it is sufficient merely to be obedient to the law of God. This seems to speak both of a certain minimalism and of a spirituality of duty. The second way of being humble is described in terms of facing options that seem to be "equally effective for the service of God our Lord and the salvation of my soul." In this kind of humility we do not desire overwhelmingly one way or another. So the second way is focused on freedom and what Ignatius calls "indifference." Interestingly, the third way of being humble, which moves beyond either duty or detachment, is described by Ignatius as "the most perfect." Here, our desire is simply to be like Christ, whatever that means in our particular circumstances. This is not so much by imitating precisely the actions of the human Jesus as recorded in scripture. Essentially it points to reaching the deepest possible level of attunement to the reality of God in me. "May they all be one, just as, Father, you are in me and I am in you, so that they also may be in us" (John 17:21).

The endpoint of the journey of discernment and choice, when we are in contact with our ultimate desire and live fully in it, is summarized in the "Contemplation to Attain Love" at the end of the *Spiritual Exercises* (Nos. 230-37). All through the process of the exercises, Ignatius Loyola has asked that we focus intently during prayer on that level of desire that

seems to be the key to the particular moment on the journey.
This reaches a climax in the "Contemplation to Attain Love"
as a desire for an all-embracing realization of and response
to God in all things.

> Here [what I desire] will be to ask for interior
> knowledge of all the great good I have received, in
> order that, stirred to profound gratitude, I may be-
> come able to love and serve the Divine Majesty in all
> things (No. 233).

It would be unrealistic to suppose that any of us lives at
this level of spiritual realization on a daily basis! But in the
"Contemplation," Ignatius offers a kind of mysticism of find-
ing God in all things to which we can aspire and which we
probably touch at moments.

Deepest Desires and God's Desiring

The process of discernment can be understood as a way
of moving from the surface of our life, the place of many
desires, to our center, our soul or our essential self, whatever
we prefer to call it. Here, where we are in contact with our
deepest desire, we find that we are essentially and simply
attuned with God.

> There is a really deep well inside us. And in it dwells
> God. Sometimes I am there too. But more often stones
> and grit block the well, and God is buried beneath.
> Then He must be dug out again (Hillesum 1985, 44).

As Etty Hillesum knew well, it would be a mistake to
pretend that this journey to our center proceeds along a
simple straight line. At different moments we move in and
out—sometimes nearer the surface of our lives, sometimes
nearer the center.

It is certain that none of us, not even people we call
saints, moves totally and finally beyond the more superficial
or even less healthy desires. We are brought back to them,

again and again. Sometimes this feels disconcerting and depressing. But in fact we never repeat things precisely in the same way. Human progress through life is rather like a spiral. It continually curls back on itself and yet is always moving deeper.

Overall, if we pursue the spiritual journey honestly and attentively, we will be able to touch our center more frequently, and its power in our lives will be more consistently released. We know those moments of being in touch with our center particularly when we have a deep well-being beyond immediate pleasures, gratifications or satisfactions. The latter, on deeper reflection, merely cloak our sense of emptiness, pain or darkness.

The journey of desire moves us beyond a sense of seeking to conform to an understanding of the "will of God" that is arbitrary and totally detached from our actual experience of living. Rather, we are drawn ever deeper into God's desiring within our lives and personalities. This is not static, predetermined or extrinsic to the kind of person we are. God's desiring in us is expressed in and through what we come to see as our deepest desires. True, this may initially be seen as in conflict with more immediately recognizable needs and wants, but God's desires in us do not conflict with our "best interests" or deepest self. The desire we seek to touch and to draw upon has been described by spiritual writers variously as the spark of God in our soul, what God has implanted in us or the truth of our being. But can we always trust our experience of desires? We can if we befriend them and then test them rather than try to ignore them or bypass them. Only then can we gradually learn how to distinguish deep desire from wants, and the "desires" that are motivated by fear from the desires that are genuinely part of a pattern of consolation.

In the end, there is no infallible *guarantee* that we will choose rightly. Ignatius Loyola reminds us of this in his comments on making an election or choice of a way of life.

When that election or decision has been made, the person who has made it ought with great diligence to go to prayer before God our Lord and to offer him that election, that the Divine Majesty may be pleased to receive and confirm it, if it is conducive to his greater service and praise (No. 183).

Our process of choosing can only be handed over to God, and the "rightness" of particular choices will be confirmed only in the long term—that is to say, within the totality of our life story. In the words of a great Methodist hymn by Charles Wesley:

Jesus, confirm my heart's desire
To work, and speak, and think for Thee;
Still let me guard the holy fire,
And still stir up Thy gift in me.

A Contemplative Experience

There is a point at which any attempt to write about desire and discernment begins to run out of vocabulary! This is precisely because what we are considering is not a skill or method but a contemplative process that leads us toward the Center that we call God. Contemplation is not static, even though the great contemplative writers often speak of waiting or stillness or being rather than doing as metaphors for the experience. Despite the assertions of some modern writers on the subject, contemplation is more than just an optional or freely chosen technique of prayer and meditation. It is an ever-deepening way of conversion, profound change and purification by fire. In it, our desires are transformed, intensified, concentrated to the point where choice, commitment and action inevitably follow.

Our difficulty with pinning down the whole business in words actually models the inconclusiveness of the process of discernment and of seeking to make our choices from the standpoint of authentic desire rather than from an easily defined "objective" and disengaged position. To enter into our desires contemplatively is to enter into a way of mystery and darkness and therefore of loss of control—and ultimately of abandonment to God.

There are several characteristics present in the experience of moving from "many desires" to the "deepest desire" out of which we seek to make life choices. One important feature is a deep and lasting contentment beyond transient pleasure. The place of deepest desire is one where we know that we are touching a deep well of peace and truthfulness that speaks of infinity—even if we have passed through disturbance and pain on the way. It is also a place where we engage with what we ultimately realize is intimately associated with our identity. That is why choices made in this place have to do with life directions rather than with the relatively trivial. Our capacity for commitment is engaged. Modern advertisers, of course, realize all this and are experts at making us think that their products do not merely satisfy some surface want but are actually vital to our identity.

To be even momentarily in our center, the place of deepest desire, is not necessarily an emotionally intense experience. However, ultimately it is recognized as an encounter with our own spirit and also with what we call God. Such experience is somehow so real that we cannot properly name it. Yet we cannot deny its validity and importance either. In its presence we are simply not able to remain unchanged with integrity or with a sense of peace. There is, in other words, a dimension of conversion involved. That is what distinguishes such experiences from insights arrived at and decisions made solely with the rational, objective mind.

This does not mean that these experiences of conversion do not need some testing. It is my experience and that of many others in spiritual ministry that increasing numbers of people seeking spiritual guidance have no extended religious background or nurture in a faith community. They are the products of conversion experiences as adults, sometimes experiences of a fairly dramatic kind. Not a few of these people in the initial intensity of the new-found desire for God assume that a vocation to ordained ministry or religious life is inevitably right. It seems a better expression of total commitment. It is vital to ask and to help people reflect whether, and to what degree, such perceptions are congruent with their whole personality and the rest of their life and experience. Often they are not.

A second characteristic of our deepest desire is that while it may be located metaphorically at the "center" of our being, it is not self-centered. It involves a movement away from isolation and introspection toward harmony or union within ourselves, with God and with all people and things. True contemplation and the process of moving inward to the depths of our desire do not isolate us from surrounding reality. It may help to consider the image of the circle. If our journey takes us to its center, and if we live and choose from that center, it becomes a point of unity, concentration and connections rather than of exclusions. It is the hub, as it were, of all desiring. The many desires of our surface consciousness, which is on the circumference of the circle, are not simply lost but discovered to be enveloped in a wholeness and inclusiveness which fulfills and completes them in an unexpected way.

A further characteristic of the search for our deepest desire is a movement from being imprisoned or overly enraptured by the multitude of apparently desirable things, toward being free to choose authentically, clearly and with integrity. There will be some point in life (or perhaps a number of points) when we come to know ourselves to be controlled or defined by many things outside ourselves—misshapen images of God, an overdeveloped sense of duty, the expectations of other people. Then there is a gradual struggle toward liberation, where we come not only to feel free to choose from the depths of our being but where God is enabled to choose in and through each of us. As one friend put it to me recently, this is an experience of really *choosing* rather than of being chosen for.

To learn how to choose freely is also to learn a great deal about dying—about letting go of much that is apparently necessary, satisfying and good in life for what is ultimately better. Such deaths happen daily. In the resurrection narrative of the Gospel of John, Mary of Magdala is confronted with the hard lesson of being asked to let go of a certain kind of human and spiritual consolation—the familiar way that Jesus has been present to her up to that point. This was in order that Jesus' mission be fulfilled. Only then could a greater good prevail for her and for the other disciples. "Do not cling to me, because I have not yet ascended to the Father" (John 20:17).

But clinging to the familiar is a natural human reaction. Somehow it is only possible to move on when we know that what is offered to us has greater potential. Classical spirituality gave the impression that we had to become detached before we could respond to God's promptings. However, my experience is that the order of events is different. We actually find ourselves being strongly attracted to something better and *then* find that we have already begun to be freed from that which held us back.

Conflicts and Blocks

Of course it would be unrealistic to pretend that the process of seeking to live out of our deepest desire is problem-free. There are clearly going to be moments when we feel a great deal of inner conflict. Is every desire I experience good in itself? Is every desire implanted in me by God? Is there ever such a thing as an evil desire? After all, the writer of Psalm 140 prays, "Do not grant the desires of the wicked, O Lord" (v. 8). These questions commonly arise in retreats and spiritual direction. They imply that there are situations in which the relatively simple distinction between desires and surface satisfactions cannot be applied easily. To a great extent these questions lie at the heart of what Ignatius Loyola teaches about the confusing spiritual experience of "temptation under the guise of good."

> It is characteristic of the evil angel, who takes on the appearance of an angel of light, to enter by going along the same way as the devout soul and then to exit by his own way with success for himself. That is, he brings good and holy thoughts attractive to such an upright soul and then strives little by little to get his own way, by enticing the soul over to his own hidden deceits and evil intentions (No. 332).

Behind this rather dated language lies the important perception that even our best motives, our capacity for great commitments, can be perverted and channelled into directions that are ultimately destructive, just as our capacity for love can be abused.

One of the most painful experiences of all arises when we find that what seems to be genuinely our heart's desire is continually hindered with apparently insuperable obstacles. This inevitably raises the question of what this is actually saying about our deepest desire. Is what we are focusing on really our deepest desire, not in the sense of most passionately held but in the sense of what is truly our ultimate concern? Are we perhaps associating a true desire with a specific way of living it out or enabling it to be realized? Are we actually choosing wholeheartedly and freely or, if the truth be known, are the obstacles that appear to be outside us or brought about by "circumstances beyond our control" still within us? The external world of events that affect us and the internal world of our own motivations and attitudes have an uncanny way of relating closely to each other.

It would be unfair to pretend that these questions always solve the dilemma. Sometimes we may have to face the mystery of "the right time" for things to happen. I have often felt myself, and frequently hear other people say, "Why didn't I do that earlier? Why couldn't I see that twenty years ago? Why has so much time been wasted?" But the reality is that we may have to wait until all kinds of inner and outer factors are in appropriate relationship. Sometimes we really can do no more than sit with the desire and the obstacles and wait for the meaning.

Hearkening Unto Myself

Ultimately, the truth of discernment and choosing lies in a patient "reposing in oneself," as Etty Hillesum put it in her diary. "And that part of myself, that deepest and richest part in which I repose, is what I call 'God.'" The work of the spirit is to "hearken unto" self, others and God.

> Truly, my life is one long hearkening unto my self and unto others, unto God. And if I say that I hearken, it is really God who hearkens inside me. The most essential and deepest in me hearkening unto the most essential and deepest in the other. God to God (Hillesum 1985, 214).

SIX

To Seek Forever:
Desire and Change

Because you are not there
When I turn, but are in the turning,
Gloria ...

... destinations are the familiarities
from which the traveller must set out ...

... What matter
if we should never arrive
to breed or to winter
in the climate of our conception?

Enough we have been given wings
and a needle in the mind
to respond to his bleak north
(Thomas 1984, "Mass for Hard Times").

Human desire can be interpreted as a permanent openness
to what is other than ourselves and to what is beyond our
boundaries. Desire is precisely a sense of incompleteness,
and therefore it becomes the condition of our openness to
possibility, to future and to the "always more," the infinite.
God always calls to us out of our future, comes to us from

our future. There is in desire something about our living in a permanently liminal state.

As body-spirit people, we naturally bridge two worlds—the world of here-and-now material reality and the "other" world, which we have traditionally called the world of the spirit. Celtic Christianity, which had such a vibrant role in Britain and Ireland, placed great importance on edges and boundaries of all kinds. These were often associated with particular geographical locations or natural features. Religious settlements of hermits or monastics sometimes gathered in such places. There were places with specific associations, such as a cemetery, which was so obviously a "passing through" place. There was, above all, the sea, which for the Celtic wanderers or "pilgrims for Christ" was not simply a route somewhere but an archetypal symbol of a deliberate spiritual displacement. It was the massive and powerful "between place" that was never far away. Here wayfarers were, like the Israelites in the desert, always "on the way." It might be said that the sea was a place of desire as the pilgrims sought above all else what they called "the place of their resurrection."

Fact of Change

Human life as a spiritual journey is a continuous process of change, a story of endings and new beginnings. Indeed, we have to come to terms with the fact that change is the norm in human life rather than the exception. The notion that knowing, stability, fixed points, being utterly clear or possessing all we need is what we should expect is questionable. Rather, movement, change and a lack of final clarity are what we live with most of the time. The other moments are occasional resting places. There is, therefore, an immense difference between linking spirituality *to* our experience of change, important though that is, and creating a spirituality *of* change, which will enable us to live within a condition of permanent transition.

The theme of death and rebirth is a recurrent one in our lives. Our experiences of loss, and even pointlessness, may later lead to a sense of new life gradually taking shape. But we cannot escape prematurely from the passages of life themselves. Indeed, our bodies insist that we take seriously the rhythms of change. For example, puberty and adolescence are inescapable. There is also no choice, ultimately, in the natural process of aging, however much we seek to hide it.

All loss is frightening, especially when it means the loss of much that has been previously valued and enjoyed. Our experience of change may be long drawn out and even agonizing. The problem is that none of us seems to be very good at radical change! We are better at clinging to the safe and known, while perhaps adjusting ourselves just a little—a kind of psychological swaying with the wind. We so often get caught up in the miseries and confusions of what we are losing. As a result, we find that we are unwilling to believe that new life is anything more than a distant promise. It is important for all of us to discover that the power of the resurrection is not something deferred but instead is present now as the key to all that is happening to us and around us.

Commenting on a spate of conversions to the Roman Catholic church by a number of prominent Anglicans, a colleague remarked that it was the desire for "a backdrop of certainty." My reaction was that even if this is true, it should not be! However, it is a fact that many of us have been brought up to expect certainty in our religious lives, or at least to think of it as the ideal. T. S. Eliot seems to have held, with Aristotle, that perfection lies in being "at rest" or still rather than in movement. Consequently, he felt ambivalent about desire, as the last few lines of "Burnt Norton" show:

Desire itself is movement
not in itself desirable;
Love is itself unmoving,
only the cause and end of movement, timeless
and undesiring,

except in the aspect of time
caught in the form of limitation
between unbeing and being.

It seems to me that a belief in absolute human certainty conflicts with the reality of desire for the infinite that is inherently part of our human condition. Desire involves openness to movement, to the fact that there is always "more" beyond our vision and grasp, to a continual potential for change. From the point of view of our present experience, the sense that we can achieve absolute certainty once and for all is a dangerous illusion.

Clearly, part of our human instinct finds the experience of uncertainty profoundly disturbing. Maybe it is to compensate for this that we tend to create a vision of life after death, specifically heaven, as a condition that will provide us with all that we feel we lack in the present life. This form of projection of our fears means that heaven is traditionally thought of as *contrasting* in all respects with our life now rather than *completing* or fulfilling it. We lose any sense of there being a profound continuity with our essential human experience in the present. An excessively therapeutic mentality in Western culture spends a great deal of time trying to deny death as much as possible. Yet because it cannot be avoided, the hope seems to be that there will be a final healing beyond death of all our ills—particularly change, movement and that very uncertainty of which death is the continual reminder.

Stages of Transition

The fact of continual change does not mean that there are no specific experiences of transition to be gone through. We cannot dictate in advance how long those experiences of transition will last. Nor can we dictate how transition will occur for each of us or on every possible occasion. We need to grow in patience and really learn to trust our experiences for what they are. There is also a right moment for particular stages of transition to come to completion. For example, we may know that it is healthy for children to leave home, and we may grow anxious about whether we are holding them back. Yet there is also a danger in being artificially doctrinaire about the timing of it all.

Even though transitions and changes are very subjective experiences for each of us, it is possible to make some general remarks and then to map out some of the more common stages. Transition marks a boundary between two situations of *relative* stability—"relative" because in reality there are no situations of complete stability and lack of movement in human life. At some level of our life and experience there is continual change and development. Our body cells change, are replaced and die all the time. In all transitions there is a movement or passage from a particular set of circumstances to another. However, the movement may, as in the parable of seed growing untended, be both hidden and prolonged.

> [Jesus] also said, "This is what the kingdom of God is like. A man scatters seed on the land. Night and day, while he sleeps, when he is awake, the seed is sprouting and growing; how, he does not know. Of its own accord the land produces first the shoot, then the ear, then the full grain in the ear. And when the crop is ready, at once he starts to reap because the harvest has come" (Mark 4:26-29).

The transition or boundary place may be where, as far as our consciousness is concerned, we can only wait. Because a process of personal change involves a shift from one life structure to another, there is obviously both a departure and an arrival. The experience of waiting can sometimes be a purging of our need for the security of the past and a place where the intensity of our desire for growth may be increased. The final departure, or letting go of what is past, has to take its time. The arrival at what is new, and the complete focus of our energies on it, cannot be complete until the ending of the previous life structure is complete. Sometimes this final ending extends over time, even while we live predominantly in the new. Perhaps for many of us, the incompleteness of our transitions is something we have to endure.

There are, as I said, a number of broad stages that seem to be common to our experiences of change and transition. Initially, the realization of a profound transition may simply immobilize us. We are struck dumb as the familiar landmarks and our normal strategies of control slip out of our grasp. Then there may be a kind of regrouping of our forces as we convince ourselves that the transition is either not happening at all or is not really all that significant. Either way, we will tend to minimize what is happening to us or pretend that our experience is not really true. The predominant feeling at this stage is relief, but it is likely to be short-lived because it is artificial.

Next we are likely to sink into depression and fear as we realize that we are being challenged more profoundly than we had hitherto anticipated. At this stage we have to go through a real stripping of illusions. Sometimes that takes us pretty deep into the darkness. It is likely to be there, in an example of paradoxical consolation, that we come to an acceptance of our present situation as "real." There then follows an important experience of letting go—at least to a degree that is sufficient to move us onward beyond the darkness. On the way forward we naturally need to test the new reality and how we should respond to it in practical terms. Our previously accepted framework of meaning and structures of commitment has been undermined in the transition, and so we need to spend time searching for what should replace them. Finally, if we continue on a healthy path, the whole experience will be internalized and will become the reality out of which we live in a committed way.

That description may be a broad overview of our experiences of transition. Someone pointed out to me that this description also fits our experiences of failure and coming to terms with it. But then, it seems to me, moments of failure are also a type of transition, as we are invited to move from protecting the self we prefer to project to acceptance of our real self.

We do need to be cautious, however. First, life is rarely as neat as our attempts to provide an overview of it! We should not fool ourselves, for example, that our lives move in straight lines or in well-ordered, successive stages where one experience or growth point can be said to be complete, over once and for all. Second, this way of describing transition can make it sound purely psychological. On a certain level it is. However, change also has a spiritual dimension that, while not absolutely distinguishable from other levels of our lives, intimately touches our sense of identity before God. It even affects our perception and acceptance of God's own identity.

The spiritual dimension of letting go and of major transitions has sometimes been described in the Christian tradition in terms of a "dark night." There is real spiritual pain that engages the level of faith as well as that of the psyche. John of the Cross, in *The Dark Night*, suggests that there is first of all a "night of sense," in which we learn to let go of familiar externals—even spiritual ones like our habitual style of prayer. Then there is a "night of the spirit," or dark night of the soul, in which we are stripped of all spiritual gratification or tangible consolation. Only then may the dawn of a new reality finally break through.

Change and Commitment

A spirituality that takes desire seriously as one of its driving forces and recognizes that change is a permanent part of the equation necessarily needs a sense of provisionality. Ultimate truth or fulfillment is never to be found in any specific *this* or *that*, whether a time, a place or a person. But a spirituality of provisionality does not contradict the ability, or indeed the need, to make commitments. Our desire is always searching for something within which to become consciously grounded—in other words, a sense of commitment.

All true commitments include risk and exclude total certainty. Anyone who has made any kind of solemn commitment or promise in private or public, including marriage or religious vows, knows this only too well. Without this balance of risk and provisionality we could not make the commitments in the first place. Nor could we make sense spiritually of the ending of relationships or the way people leave particular contexts of commitment after many years. It is difficult, too, to make sense even of the fact that there are natural endings within human commitments; for example, when our children leave home or our partner dies. Provisionality enables us to make sense of faithfulness and continuity (our own and God's) within the risk of commitment and, at the same time, in these experiences of painful change.

In reality we can only discern the truth of our desires and the focus of our commitments at any given moment as best we can, that is, provisionally. At some point we need to stop equivocating and choose to risk a commitment. Even though I was brought up by the ocean, I still tend to hesitate before diving into water of any kind. I fear the shock of the cold. But in the end I cannot decide what the water might be like to swim in simply by sitting on the rocks and wondering! The problem with commitment is that it is not static or fully realized in the moment of first decision. Commitment is itself a journey.

We are right if we think that human commitments are dangerous because unpredictable, and balk slightly at the prospect. Perhaps, we sometimes think, it would be kinder to ourselves and to others not to enter such uncertain territory. This is particularly true if we have been taught that commitment depends on our own will power and effort, and that once we have made a visible commitment we have an absolute duty to remain faithful to all its surrounding circumstances. "You've made your bed, so lie on it!" The catch is that if we try to defend ourselves with all kinds of qualifying clauses in our heads before we undertake any commitment, it ends up being no commitment at all.

It helps to know that it is a mysterious God at the heart of our mysterious selves that forms the level of deepest commitment, to which our desires draw us, and to which we need to remain faithful if we are to remain whole. It also helps to know the difference between this level of commitment and the human, particular, necessary and yet contingent contexts within which we try to live out this commitment at any one point in time. Our commitments always need to be properly grounded and embodied in specific contexts or relationships, but it would be false to pretend that any human embodiment is absolute. The experiences of commitment and choice, therefore, have two dimensions. First, we need to be wholeheartedly engaged. But second, in terms of the human contexts within which we express them, commitments are always a risk and are always, therefore, provisional.

Like love itself, the experience of being drawn toward our deepest desire, and having it unfold before us, can be testing, stressful and rather like sailing in uncharted seas. It is hard to remain true to this sense of being called, of being drawn into a mysterious and deeper truth when it involves, as it often does, shedding the security of many familiar landmarks and assumptions. The most profound test of our trust in God, as well as of our own resolve, occurs when this sense of call initially appears to confuse the people we love and respect, to contradict some of our long-standing loyalties and ties, and to appear "irrational." The directions set by love and the search for an inner integrity frequently do not correspond to the canons of "the sensible."

Conversion

The traditional monastic vow of *conversatio morum,* "conversion of manners," speaks of a commitment to permanent change and therefore vulnerability. Insofar as our baptismal call is to live within the power of the resurrection, this vulnerability is entirely appropriate. An important icon of risen life has Jesus present to his disciples with open wounds. Woundedness retains its depth even if transfigured and glorified.

Although we think of monasticism primarily in terms of stability, a desire for and commitment to change as a condition of living is also central to the Rule of St. Benedict. The early desert fathers and mothers recommended to their disciples, "Stay in your cell and it will teach you everything." Clearly it is important not to run away from where our struggles are based. That is what stability implies. Yet, at the same time we are always people who must desire to move on. This *conversatio*, conversion, implies a radical response on our part to Jesus' words, "Come, follow me." We need stability, but we also need to live provisionally and to travel light.

The call to change also means that we and our desires are continually confronted with the challenge to be converted and to choose between reality and unreality. Just as change is a process not a moment, so conversion is an unfolding state of mind and heart rather than a static or self-contained point. The God who is at the heart of change and to whom we are converted ultimately eludes us. There is always a new aspect. Whatever illumination we receive, we are always left at a new "square one." However, there is a consistent temptation to turn aside from the search for a true vision of God and to settle for one aspect, one face of God, and call it "all." We try to capture the fullness of God in one moment, and then to hold on to the moment.

The danger of so-called conversion experiences, particularly in our consumer culture, is that the language we use can give the impression that the task has been fully accomplished. We will now live happily ever after; we have arrived at a condition of rest that is human perfection. But in fact, the reality is not like this and everything is not under control. Conversion is more likely to mean that things,

perhaps for the first time in our lives, get out of control. To
be transfigured like Jesus we need to die. But real dying
involves losing the illusion of control. That is why it is such
a struggle. Conversion is always to another state of
provisionality rather than a simple movement from chaos
and uncertainty to the rock of final invulnerability.

The goal of the spiritual journey, God, is ever-expanding
as far as our perceptions are concerned. The experience is not
a commodity called "perfection" but a process of being continually filled. It involves responsiveness rather than grasping. For this, we have to give up the search for the horizons
we find humanly so necessary—especially tangible progress
and visible success. Conversion leads us to respond only to
the "coordinates of grace" rather than to expectations, our
own or other people's. As Angela Tilby, a British television
producer and theologian, said recently:

> I don't think there is a grounding in this time of chaos
> other than the willingness to free-fall or float-free,
> with the shards of our shattered images of God, each
> other, our selves, as space dust around us.

So, conversion is a time of chaos, searching and the loss
of paradigms. Yet it is, at the same time, a period of choice
and of creativity. In its spiritual dimension true conversion
involves both grieving and celebration. As with all change,
there is a turning away from something and a turning to a
new direction. Too often the popular language of conversion
experiences sounds as if all conversion is from sin to grace,
from bad things to good things. This is too black and white,
and it also gives the impression that conversion is essentially
only a moral question. As one elderly priest said in a rather
powerful homily, "I have found that the hardest thing is not
to choose between good and bad but between what is good
and what is better."

Without entering into the complexities of theological
debate about the nature of conversion, there are a number of
things that may be said about it in relation to desire and

change. First, conversion is neither purely intellectual (a change of mind) nor is it purely moral (a change of behavior). From the religious perspective, conversion has a certain emotional quality because it is tied up with our desire for God and for ultimate spiritual completion as persons. There is also a profundity to conversion that moves it beyond a merely routine shift of behavior, an increase of knowledge or decision to join some new institution or group of people.

The profound changes that can validly be described in terms of conversion engage our commitment, ultimately of every dimension of ourselves, head, heart, psyche and spirit. While we may have difficulty in speaking of Jesus being "converted" in a moral sense, it is certainly possible to speak of the "conversion" of Jesus in a broader sense. Jesus undoubtedly had to face a crisis of meaning and identity in his life, and he responded to it by rethinking his relationship to God, his Father. There are two key texts here, which follow on from each other in the narratives of the synoptic gospels: Jesus' baptism in the Jordan and his temptations in the wilderness (Matthew 3:13-4:11; Mark 1:9-13; Luke 3:21-22; 4:1-13). The whole sequence acts, as it were, as a process of conversion. In the unconditional acceptance of Jesus by God in his baptism there was a true call. This is followed by Jesus' acceptance of his mission and a reordering of his priorities, of which the temptations story provides a powerful symbol. The wilderness narratives in particular offer a classic expression of the free surrender of a sense of absolute autonomy as well as of a denial of those self-serving desires that interfere with a single-minded commitment to God in love.

In later Christian tradition, many people would single out St. Augustine's *Confessions* as the classic conversion text. Although a turning from sin (*metanoia* or repentance) is involved, this is not the whole story. Nor is St. Augustine's account simply of a philosophical conversion in the sense of some conclusion to a search for intellectual truth. St. Augustine's conversion was an experience of inner transformation that had a great deal to do with desire. Indeed, it may be seen as the transformation of St. Augustine's desire from being directed to self-satisfaction to a powerfully focused yearning for God.

In a sense, the conversions of both the human Jesus and of St. Augustine center around love and desire. Both the human Jesus and St. Augustine sought and struggled with the call to love without limits. In both human loving and our love of God, the conversion process is one of "decentering," that is, of moving beyond seeing the self as the unquestioned center of reality. The deep change that is involved in conversion is a radical surrender, but a surrender in *love*. Only falling in love, both with another person and with God, makes it possible for us to surrender the self to any significant degree at all.

Desire and Journey

The experience of conversion and the process of change has been particularly symbolized in the Jewish and Christian traditions by "wilderness" in its various forms. There was the desert of the Israelites and the early Christian hermits, and the sea of the Celtic wanderers. In contrast (and partly unfairly, without doubt) the temptation to settle too readily and too fully has been symbolized by the city.

There is a tension in the Hebrew tradition between a sense that the desert wanderings recounted in the Exodus narrative were the time and place of a true encounter with God, and the sense that God and God's promise were powerfully present in the particular place of the Chosen Land. In the desert there was no abiding city, merely a God who continually called the people onward to new places of encounter, which could only be reached by faithfulness to God alone. Yet the land is a central theme of biblical faith. This land of promise was *the* sign of the covenant between God and the people. Eventually Zion, Jerusalem, and especially the Temple became associated in a special way with God's presence.

So, two theologies existed side by side in the Hebrew scriptures, sometimes uncomfortably so. The theology of the "Moses" school of thinking was always sharply aware of the spiritual temptations of settling down and becoming too fixed in our ways. The experience of wandering, of desiring but never totally arriving, of complete trust in God, was central. The contrasting theology of the "King David" school reflected the experience of coming into possession of the land, of settlement and of developing a Temple cult. The desert was an ambiguous symbol of trial and tribulation that did eventually come to an end in the fulfillment of God's promise to bring the descendants of Abraham into possession of the land.

The founding scriptures of Christianity are deeply embedded in the Jewish experience of defeat, exile and ceasing to be a nation that was inextricably linked to a special sacred landscape. Much of the writing of the Christian scriptures was born in the Jewish diaspora. This gave early Christianity a context in which spiritually to some degree, as well as physically, it moved away from its roots in the daily life of Jesus and the early disciples in rural Palestine. Eventually it became a faith that expanded through missionary journeying throughout the breadth of the Roman Empire. The theology is of a people on the move. Christians are "people of the way." The most characteristic lifestyle of the recorded heroes is the journey. The whole of this present life was considered to be fragile, a liminal moment prior to the final dramatic arrival of God's Kingdom.

One of the later Christian traditions that picked up this theme of movement and journey and turned it into a focus for spiritual desire was the Celtic, especially the Irish, one. "We stole away because we wanted for the love of God to be on pilgrimage, we cared not whither." In this way, according to the Anglo-Saxon Chronicle of 891, some Irish monks spoke to King Alfred after they had landed in Cornwall in a boat without a rudder. Wandering for the love of God caused astonishment and admiration. The development of *peregrinatio*, wandering exile, was one of the most extraordinary aspects of Irish spirituality. For five hundred years Irish pilgrims left homeland, friends, security, certainties and stability and set out for the unknown, desiring to be totally trusting in God.

In one of his sermons St. Columbanus, one of the greatest of Irish wanderers, preached that all Christians are to be *hospites mundi*, "guests of the world":

> It is the end of the road that travellers look for and desire, and because we are travellers and pilgrims through this world, it is the road's end, that is of our lives, that we should always be thinking about.

The key was not just change, journeying and movement in themselves, but "to seek the place of our resurrection." The outer journey was a powerful symbol of the inner journey of deep desire to be in harmony with the sacred—the same inner journey undertaken by the Celtic solitaries who never left their homeland:

> Alone in my little oratory without a single human being in my company; dear to me would such a pilgrimage be before going to meet death (Murphy 1956, no. 9).

To journey physically simply indicated acceptance of a permanent condition of change or transition in life and in relation to everything around. It focused human desire away from settling for a mere *this* or *that*. By letting go of all the things, places and people that they held dear, the Celtic wanderers sought to root out all desires that were for less than all. The conditions of the Celtic ascetics may have been extreme and their behavior very radical if not positively foolhardy, but the wanderers remind us in a romantic and dramatic way of the inner journey of desire that all Christians are called to undertake.

Desire and Eternity

Are the experiences we have in this world of uncertainty, change and journeying meant inevitably to lead our desire in the direction of an eternity of changeless certainty? Or, on the contrary, have we missed the point if we think the present is disconnected from and merely the waiting room for a future "real" life? Is it, perhaps, the case that the continually changing quality of our present life does not so much point to the next world as a kind of compensation as suggest our need to be purged now of a misleading desire for a final moment of completion and full possession of God?

This has a great deal to do with our image of God and of our essential self in relation to God. Is God beyond time, eternally the same and immune from change of any kind? In a world of flux and change do we not need the stability of God? Is that what heaven and being with God means for us as well? I am not at all sure that our affirmation of relationships within God (Trinity) and God's engagement with us in love (creation and incarnation) make it possible to eliminate all notion of change from God. The dynamic quality of God-in-Trinity, who is being-in-relationship, points to a dynamic rather than static view of eternity. Change and response rather than changelessness express the being of God, whose nature is to be vulnerable in love.

The God who is at the heart of change always ultimately eludes us.

He is such a fast God,
always before us and
leaving as we arrive (Thomas 1984, "Pilgrimages").

There is always a new aspect to this God. Every definition we arrive at and every spiritual experience we think of as definitive merely becomes another "square one." We are ever having to begin the journey again with God although, equally, we are always tempted to turn aside from the vision that feeds our insatiable desire and to settle for one seemingly comforting aspect of God.

To live with the true God eternally will be an experience of non-possession, the provisionality of all our perceptions, and will always contain an element of unknowing in that our affirmation of God will never be complete, *be* God. It seems to me, therefore, that we can talk of perpetual change in our knowledge of God and can say that desire will always be a force that is integral to our relationship with God.

I am not sure that death promises us the end of time in every sense. What is spoken of by the Christian tradition is the end of *temporality*. This does not strike me as the same thing at all. *Temporality* implies loss, decay and the passing away of things. *Eternity*, whatever it might mean, does not seem to imply sheer timelessness, even if it may involve transcending, in some kind of simultaneous vision, the limitations of our experience of time as merely successive and utterly distinct moments.

Yet, for St. Augustine, when desire achieves its goal in heaven, perfect knowledge follows. For heavenly knowledge and desire are of the same reality: God who is love. True wisdom, tasted but not fulfilled in this material life, is "the knowledge and love of him who always is, and never changes, namely God" ("Homily on Psalm 135:8"). All in all, St. Augustine's understanding of desire and knowledge seems to add up to the notion that the enjoyment of heaven will totally satisfy our desire to know and to love. However, this static understanding of eternal life is balanced by other texts. Interestingly, St. Augustine asks whether, if we will be eternally loving God, we will also be eternally seeking God. His response is that just as our love for a friend who is close at hand in this life grows, so our love of God in heaven will always grow. "As love grows, the search for the one who has been found also increases" ("Homily on Psalm 104:3").

What drives the whole process of existence for a human being is the desire for God, that is, eros. This implies a perpetual and not accidental process of growth and change.

Love is always dynamic because it is never completed. It is always incomplete because it is forever open to new "revelation" about the one who is loved. Love is always open to new things because at no point does it possess the other. With God, especially, we can never talk about grasping or finally naming God. There is a paradox in St. Augustine's notion that our hearts ultimately find *rest* in God. If it is rest, it is not because our heart's desire is dimmed.

The early Eastern theologian Gregory of Nyssa also seems to argue that our desire for God inherently involves a perpetual movement.

> Certainly whoever pursues true virtue participates in nothing other than God, because he is himself absolute virtue. Since, then, those who know what is good by nature desire participation in it, and since this good has no limit, the participant's desire itself necessarily has no stopping place but stretches out with the limitless (*Life of Moses*, Book 1.7).

> Every desire for the Good which is attracted to that ascent constantly expands as one progresses in pressing on to the Good (Book 2.238).

> This truly is the vision of God: never to be satisfied in the desire to see him. But one must always, by looking at what he can see, rekindle his desire to see more. Thus, no limit would interrupt growth in the ascent to God, since no limit to the Good can be found nor is the increasing of desire for the Good brought to an end because it is satisfied (Book 2.239).

For Gregory, perfection lies in continual progress rather than in some static completion. Equally, while there may be a "true" vision of God, it is nevertheless the case that all possible visions of God are deficient in relation to what God fully is. So God appears to Gregory to say "the place with me is so great that the one running in it is never able to cease from his progress" (Book 2.242).

What we speak of as heaven or being with God for all eternity is the final goal of what writers such as Gregory of Nyssa understood by the mystical ascent to God that was the call of every Christian as the result of baptism. In the powerful words of the French thinker, the late Michel de Certeau, mystical experience is to be caught up in "an eternity without shores." Because God has no shoreline, as it were, the desiring of our hearts will also, I believe, prove to be of infinite extent and duration.

> He or she is a mystic who cannot stop walking and, with the certainty of what is lacking, knows of every place and object that it is *not that*; one cannot stay *there* nor be content with *that*. Desire creates an excess. Places are exceeded, passed, lost behind it. It makes one go further, elsewhere. It lives nowhere (De Certeau 1992, 299).

References

Aelred of Rievaulx. 1977. *Spiritual Friendship*. Kalamazoo: Cistercian Publications.

Augustine. *Confessions*. There are several modern editions.

Bonaventure. 1978. *The Soul's Journey into God*. New York: Paulist Press.

Catherine of Siena. 1980. *The Dialogue*. New York: Paulist Press.

Cloud of Unknowing, The. 1981. New York: Paulist Press.

de Certeau, Michel. 1992. *The Mystic Fable*. Chicago: University of Chicago Press.

Donne, John. 1971. *Poetical Works*. Oxford: University Press.

Dillard, Annie. 1977. *Pilgrim at Tinker Creek*. New York: Harper Collins.

Eckhart, Meister. 1986. *Teacher and Preacher*. New York: Paulist Press.

—————. 1981. *The Essential Sermons, Commentaries, Treatises and Defense*. New York: Paulist Press.

Ecclestone, Alan. 1975. *Yes to God*. London: Darton, Longman & Todd.

Eliot, T. S. 1963. *Collected Poems*. New York: Harcourt Brace.

Gregory of Nyssa. 1978. *The Life of Moses*. New York: Paulist Press.

Hadewijch. 1981. *The Complete Works*. New York: Paulist Press.

Hill, Susan. 1992. *Air and Angels*. London: Mandarin.

Hillesum, Etty. 1985. *An Interrupted Life*. New York: Washington Square Press.

Hudgins, Andrew. 1991. *The Never-Ending*. Boston: Houghton Mifflin Company.

Ignatius of Loyola. 1992. *The Spiritual Exercises*. Chicago: Loyola University Press.

John of the Cross. 1987. *Selected Writings*. New York: Paulist Press.

Julian of Norwich. 1978. *Showings*. New York: Paulist Press.

Murphy, Gerard. 1956. *Early Irish Lyrics*. Oxford: University Press.

Peers, E. Allison. 1950. *The Complete Works of St. Teresa of Jesus*. Volume 2. New York: Sheed and Ward.

Pseudo-Dionysius. 1987. *The Complete Works*. New York: Paulist Press.

Rilke, Rainer Maria. 1954. *Letters to a Young Poet*. New York: W. W. Norton & Co.

Sobrino, Jon. 1978. *Christology at the Crossroads*. Maryknoll, NY: Orbis Books.

Solovyov, Vladimir. 1945. *The Meaning of Love*. London: The Centenary Press.

Teresa of Avila. 1979. *The Interior Castle*. New York: Paulist Press.

Tillich, Paul. 1963. *Systematic Theology*. Volume 3. Chicago: University of Chicago Press.

_____ . 1955. *The New Being*. New York: Charles Schribner's.

_____ . 1954. *Love, Power and Justice*. New York: Oxford University Press.

Thomas, R. S. 1992. *Mass for Hard Times*. Newcastle upon Tyne: Bloodaxe Books.

_____. 1984. *Later Poems*. London: Macmillan.

Traherne, Thomas. 1991. *Selected Poems & Prose*. London: Penguin Books.

_____. 1975. *Centuries*. London: Mowbray.

Ward, Benedicta, ed. 1975. *The Sayings of the Desert Fathers*. Kalamazoo, MI: Cistercian Publications.

Wilber, Ken. 1991. *Grace and Grit: Spirituality and Healing in the Life and Death of Treya Killam Wilber*. Boston: Shambala.